Pregnancy to Playtime

Unlock your Inner Dad Hero

2-in-1 Dad Collection

BRAD WELLS

TABLE OF CONTENTS

PREGNANCY GUIDE FOR DADS

A COMPLETE HANDBOOK FOR MEN BECOMING FIRST- TIME FATHERS

BRAD WELLS

within this book has been derived from various sources. Please consult a licensed professional before attempting any techniques outlined in this book.

By reading this document, the reader agrees that under no circumstances is the author responsible for any losses, direct or indirect, that are incurred as a result of the use of the information contained within this document, including, but not limited to, errors, omissions, or inaccuracies.

INTRODUCTION

I remember those months after getting married as the ones with the most vivid dreams I've ever had. Debbie and I had enjoyed our intimate wedding reception. We headed for a brief honeymoon at Niagara Falls, looking forward to what we had planned as our biggest adventure: trying for a baby and starting our family. The idea of becoming a father had impregnated not only my daily thoughts but also my subconscious! And so, every morning, I wokeup recalling images of the weirdest dreams:

- I dreamed of caring for a litter of talking kittens; they were all hungry, and their little squeaks made me desperate.

- I was walking hand in hand with Mickey Mouse and other cartoon characters.

- Debbie was stranded on a desert island. I had to reach her by swimming against the current, but the waters kept pushing me farther and farther.

- The baby was already born. Debbie handed her to me, and as I held her, I realized that she was entirely made of glass.

You get the picture, right? And the day Debbie showed me the pregnancy test with those two pink strips, my dreams only got weirder and more vivid. I was thrilled about having a baby with the woman I loved. I was excited about becoming a dad. But also, I was terrified! I felt like I had no clue about what was going on inside her body. Every little symptom had me reaching out to my mother and big sister—this was back in the old days when Google wasn't a thing! I was concerned about her health, about the baby's well-being, about labor, and more than anything, I kept wondering whether I was going to be up to the task. Was I dad material after all? How was I going to provide for my family and be a part of the baby's life at the same time? How could I make sure my wife felt taken care of and understood if I didn't understand the whole pregnancy thing?

To make things even worse, I was reluctant to open up with any of my friends back then. I believed that talking about my fears and worries wasn't manly and that they might think pregnancy is a woman's thing. Fortunately, this isn't likely your case. My older daughter is in her mid-20s; yours is a whole new world!

MILLENNIAL DADS AND THEIR STRUGGLES

Nowadays, more dads than ever before are embracing an active role right from the start: Gender roles have become flexible, and men are encouraged to participate in every step of the journey.

According to *Pew Research*, millennial dads spend as much as three times the hours with their children than the previous generation of fathers (Livingston & Parker, 2019). No more old-fashioned pictures of dads waiting in the hospital lobby smoking cigars, thank you! Dads today are present at childbirth, changing diapers, bottle-feeding, providing support to breastfeeding moms, and making conscious decisions about education, parenting styles, discipline, and such.

While all this is good news, it also means you may feel more pressure than fathers of previous generations: You know you have a significant role to embrace, which may cause you worries, fears, and concerns. You may feel unprepared to fit this role, and you don't want to overwhelm your partner with your doubts—she's already going through a lot! You may be coping with stress, anxiety, or even depression. Pregnancy and fatherhood cause a sudden shift in your identity as well as in your relationship.

You know that family comes first in your list of priorities, and nothing is more important to you than your partner's healthy pregnancy and delivery. At the same time, you can't help but worry about financial issues: How will you pay for hospital bills, diapers, daycare, and everything else? How can you make sure you balance work-life responsibilities?

Once your baby is born, you may feel better. At least now you can take the matter into your own hands, right? Well... that's what you think until you discover the impressive amount of time newborns spend breastfeeding! Talk about feeling useless, huh? You may struggle to connect with your baby and find that your partner is a whole new person, and you can't easily communicate with hereither. You are going through a lot, but you feel you have to bottle up for the sake of your marriage!

Last but not least, while there's plenty of information available online today, you may find mixed messages and become even more confused. Navigating the healthcare system is not easy, especially when it's your first time. You need support and guidance to overcome your confusion.

WHAT YOU' LL LEARN FROM THIS BOOK

After four healthy pregnancies and five babies—our youngest are twins!—I feel confident as a dad, although there are new challenges as children grow. I've been in your place, and I wrote this book thinking about what I would have loved to read back when I was young, scared, and inexperienced, but eager to learn and become the best possible dad I knew my new family deserved.

In the following chapters, we'll approach what I like to call the CRAFT method: It will enable you to prepare yourself for each step of the amazing pregnancy journey you are about to start or maybe are already walking through.

What does CRAFT stand for? Consider, Recognize, Awareness, Fatherhood, and Time.

Consider: This will give you a glimpse of what it's like to be a parent and help you determine if you're ready.

Recognize: This step helps you recognize the signs of pregnancy.

Awareness: This step is about getting information (explanation and details about pregnancy), advice, and tips you'll need as you expect the new family member.

Fatherhood: Here, you'll find helpful advice and hacks to help you ease into your new role as a dad.

Time: Finally, this step reminds you of the need for self- care and time with your partner as you parent your child.

After reading this book, I hope you'll feel empowered, confident, and ready to enjoy the fantastic journey you and your partner are about to live. I'm not here to tell you how to love your baby. You already have what it takes to be a great dad. Read this book to rejoice in the process! And if you can learn something in the meantime, even better.

Are you feeling excited yet? Then, let's get started!

TAKE TIME TO CONSIDER

A couple I met—let's call them Daniel and Juliet—were enjoying the newlywed life. They have just bought a new car and love driving to places during the weekends. Both were focused on their careers and didn't feel obliged to start a family right away. However, everything changed after being invited to the birthday party of one of Daniel's nephews. People began asking them if they had any children, and every time they said "no," they added the word "yet." After all, babies *were* part of their plan, and suddenly, they felt they couldn't wait to get one! Especially since they spend hours looking at other people's babies at the party.

Babies are cute! Their rosy cheeks, their big bright eyes, their chubby legs... It's Mother Nature's trick to ensure we care for them even if they aren't our own. But no matter how much you love babies, deciding to have one isn't something to take lightly. After all, fatherhood is a lifelong commitment. You and your partner should take time to evaluate whether you are ready for this new chapter in your life and your relationship.

IS IT BABY FEVER OR IS IT TIME?

Being surrounded by all those cute little nephews and nieces in their baby outfits, smelling like lavender and roses, and smiling at the birthday balloons during that party, Daniel and Juliet got baby fever. Perhaps you've heard the term before, but is it actually a thing? "Baby fever" describes the sudden urge or desire to have a baby. More than a real phenomenon, it's a colloquial term used to explain the emotion of wanting a child.

How you experience babies around you may influence whether you get a baby fever or not. Believe me: After a six-hour flight next to a crying baby, you may find yourself more likely to get a vasectomy than having a baby. But don't worry! Baby fever is unrelated to your suitability for being a parent: If you've never experienced baby fever and you find out your partner is pregnant, you can still be a fantastic dad! Maybe you get baby fever only after you meet your actual baby, and that's okay.

Some people put a lot of pressure on others—especially women— based on the supposedly ticking biological clock. A woman in her 30s who still hasn't had children is likely to be asked several times why she doesn't have a baby yet. This question causes more harm than good, so refrain from asking it next time! People have allkinds of reasons for not having children. Maybe their financialsituation isn't the best; perhaps they have some unresolved health issues they need to sort out before—it can be as simple as having a wisdom tooth removed or as complex as going through fertility treatment—or maybe they aren't *quite there* yet.

If you and your partner are wondering whether it's time to try for a baby, put aside society's expectations. There's a common myth from the 1970s that says women experience a sudden decline in their fertility cliff after 35. Today, we know this isn't necessarily true, and many factors influence the capacity to carry a healthy pregnancy (such as smoking, previous health conditions, and life habits). Women are having healthy children at age 40 or beyond. Besides, fertility issues aren't necessarily a woman's thing: In one- third of the cases, the problem is with the man (Gouza, 2022).Fortunately, these problems can often be treated.

In a few words, the decision to get pregnant should not be based on what others expect. It's something only you and your partner should decide. Having a baby is a lifelong commitment. Don't let statistics, relatives, or even doctors pressure you. Open, honest conversations with your partner are the best way to tell if the time has come.

A GLIMPSE OF PARENTHOOD

After flying home after the family gathering, Daniel and Juliet start discussing the possibility of trying to get pregnant. They are aware that their lives will be transformed by becoming parents. However, they still need to evaluate the extent of this profound transformation before deciding whether they are ready to try to conceive.

First of all, I suggest you assess your relationship. A baby should never be the glue that holds the two of you together when you're otherwise falling apart! Starting a family should be a shared project when you are comfortable and happy with each other. Although it's the biggest adventure and you will grow strongerthan ever, a baby can also shake your foundations. Believe me,some days you will look at each other and want to run far, far away—but if the couple is strong enough, you'll overcome the obstacles anyway.

Before trying to conceive, you should both have a medical check-up. I'm sure you know already that health is a significant issue when it comes to trying to get pregnant, but even if you are adopting, you should also consider your mental health. Postpartum depression is a common condition that can also affect fathers. Make sure you have a strong support system and that you areaware of any signs. We'll further discuss this issue in Chapters 7 and 8.

There are financial considerations to take into account. For a start, a baby significantly impacts a household budget. Supposing you already have proper house accommodations and a car big enough to fit a stroller on the trunk, you'll spend on diapers, baby wipes, formula, doctors, health and life insurance, vaccines, daycare, safety devices, and so on. In the long term, you must evaluate more considerable expenses such as education. You and your partner should decide on issues such as parental leave, savings, and childcare options.

Although poopy diapers may scare you now, they are nothing compared to what lies ahead of your parenting journey! Parental responsibilities are legal obligations that bind you to your children until they are old and mature enough to provide for themselves. It's not enough to keep your kids healthy, fed, and dressed. Your responsibilities only increase as your baby grows up and becomes a child. As a parent, you must be ready to make unpopular decisions and keep your children safe, but at the same time, you must teach them to function independently, hold them accountable, support them emotionally, and make sure they develop values that align with yours.

After some weeks and many long talks, Daniel and Juliet decide they are ready to try. They embrace the many changes having a baby will bring into their lives and face the future with optimism while accepting they still have a few things to figure out. Just like them, you, too, will be profoundly changed by becoming a dad.

Although fatherhood is different for every family, and not every person gets equally involved or experiences it in the same way, here are a few ways your life is likely to change:

- **Your daily routine:** At first, you may feel you have no free time. Your baby will take up all your physical and mental energy, and you may even find that your whole identity is reshaped by becoming a father. You may need to work longer hours to provide for your family, take up new household duties, or probably both! And forget about having drinks with the guys after office; you'll need to rushhome to cook dinner—or maybe you will hardly wait to get to bed after those long nights of sleep deprivation.

- **Your brain and hormones:** Although the physical impact of becoming a dad isn't as noticeable as the one women experience, having a baby also changes men's bodies. Unlike what happens in women, who experience changes from the moment of conception, in men, these physical transformations aren't directly related to the biological event of becoming a father but to their level of commitment and how much they participate in caring for their newborn. Researchers discovered men experience higher levels of oxytocin and lower testosterone the more involved they are in childcare. Their brains also transform the areas responsible for empathy, nurturing, and emotional response (LoMonaco, 2022). Those hormonal changes promote a deeper bond between the father and the baby, so they are welcome!

- **Your partner's life:** A woman's life is deeply transformed by the whole process of conceiving, being pregnant, delivering a baby, and possibly breastfeeding for a long time. Her changing body will be the most minor surprise! You may feel you don't recognize your partner as she becomes emotional and vulnerable, but at the same time, stronger than ever before. Your relationship will go through changes as well. Every aspect, from your sex life to your long-term goals and priorities, is likely to be shaken.

- **Your relationship with others:** When you become a dad, your whole social circle will likely change. Some childless friends may disappear into the mist, but you'll also make new friends in unexpected places, such as the playground or daycare. Your relationship with your parents will be reshaped as they become grandparents. For a while, I believed my mom had forgotten that I existed since she only had eyes for her delightful grandchild!

- **Your baby's life:** You are bringing a new human being onto the planet. It's your decision, not theirs! Therefore, you need to fully embrace your responsibilities regarding their physical, mental, and emotional well-being.

As you can see, having a baby isn't a decision to be taken lightly. I don't mean to scare you. Despite all those changes, in the end, you will feel there's nothing you'd rather have chosen in the world when you hold your baby's hand for the first time.

QUIZ: ARE YOU READY TO BECOME A DAD?

Here's a little questionnaire that may help you and your partner decide whether you are ready to embrace the responsibility of becoming a dad. I invite you to take the quiz together. Write down your answers and check. Some questions may be a bit awkward, but it's always best to find out before the baby is on the way. In any case, it's not supposed to be taken too seriously but to work as a starting point for important conversations and set clear expectations.

- Why do we want to have a baby precisely now? What are we willing to do if pregnancy doesn't happen right away? Are we set for medical bills? How will we pay for prenatal studies, labor, hospital stays, and pediatricians?

- How will we divide the housework during pregnancy and after the baby is born? Who will get up at night to feed the baby?

- Do our current jobs offer parental leave? Who is going to take it, and for how long? Who is going to look after the baby afterward?

- How do we picture ourselves as mom or dad? How do we want to parent? What do we like about our upbringing, and what would we like to do differently with our child? How will we handle stress and conflict resolution? What are our ideas of discipline?

- How will we make time for the relationship once the baby is born? How will we get personal time? How will we handle self-care?

- Are we going to raise our children in a religion? Which values do we want to pass on?

- How do we picture the future as a family? Which role will grandparents and other extended family members have in our lives?

IT' S NOT ALWAYS EASY AS IT SEEMS

When Juliet and Daniel finally decided they were ready to try, the first thing they did was to stop using contraceptive methods. Much to their surprise, a few months later, there was still no baby! Daniel confessed to me that he felt doubt and frustration: "You spend all of your 20s taking measures not to get a girl pregnant, and all of a sudden, it's all you've ever wanted," he said, "and when it doesn't happen, you wonder if there's something wrong with you!"

Sometimes, pressure and anxiety get in the way of a perfectly healthy couple conceiving a child. While teenagers and young people believe pregnancy just happens—hey, it *can* happen, so by all means, if you don't want to become a father just yet, you should stick to birth control—the reality is that for many couples, it takes longer than expected. About 80% of heterosexual couples conceive after six months of trying, and about 90% within a year. If it hasn't happened to you yet, maybe it's simply because you haven't tried long enough!

Also, keep in mind that for pregnancy to happen, sexual intercourse should be well-timed with ovulation. There are many apps available to track your fertility window and plan your pregnancy

—although, yes, it takes away some spontaneity from romance and love-making.

However, if you have unsuccessfully attempted to get pregnant for six months to a year, it's advisable to check with a doctor. Before worrying about medical problems, they'll evaluate specific risk factors that can get in the way of fertility, such as:

- smoking, drinking alcohol, or using recreational drugsliving with chronic stress or not getting enough sleep being significantly over or underweight

- having an underlying medical condition, such as diabetes,a thyroid imbalance, or an undiagnosed sexually transmitted disease (STD)

- having been through cancer treatment in the past taking certain prescribed medications

If the couple is younger than 35 and has been unsuccessfully trying to conceive for a year, doctors speak about infertility. It has multiple causes, such as, in women, an obstruction in the fallopian tube, an ovulation disorder, or abnormalities in the uterus such as endometriosis; and in men, sperm disorders such as a low sperm count, low motility, or sperm abnormally shaped. Blocked or swollen veins in the scrotum can cause these problems. Premature ejaculation or erectile dysfunction can also make it difficult to impregnate your partner.

Most infertility causes don't have any symptoms. Therefore, doctors need to perform specific tests to discover why a couple can't conceive. An infertility evaluation consists of several assessments, such as:

- a physical examination

- a detailed review of your medical history

- blood tests to check the thyroid and hormone levels and rule out any possible STD

- imagining exams of the woman's fallopian tubes and uterus

- a semen analysis

Unlike previous generations, now we know infertility isn't a woman's thing. In 20%-30% of cases, it's the male partner who has the fertility problem. In another astounding 40%, both partners have factors. So, forget about the bias about women not being able to get pregnant. Make sure both of your doctors know you are trying to conceive and that you are both tested.

Sometimes, the causes of infertility can be tracked, and other times, it remains unexplained, but almost always, it can be treated. The options depend on the results of the evaluation. For example, if infertility is traced to an underlying medical condition, such as an obstruction in a fallopian tube or a blocked vein in the scrotum, surgery can fix the problem. Other times, fertility might be restored with medication. Advanced treatments include intrauterine insemination (IUI) or in-vitro fertilization (IVF). Eachtreatment has pros and cons; some are more invasive than others, and each journey through pregnancy or parenthood is unique, somake sure you discuss your options with your doctor.

After their first appointment with the specialist, Daniel and Juliet found out it was normal for many couples not to get pregnant right away. They felt relieved to find out there were so many options available. They scheduled the first tests of their fertility evaluation, but there was no need for any. The following month, they got positive on their home pregnancy test. Their journey had begun!

KEY TAKEAWAYS

We've seen the importance of having long, honest conversations with your partner to assess whether you are ready to try for a baby beyond societal pressures and momentary "baby fever." We've also considered the many ways your life will transform once you become a father. And we've also learned that pregnancy may not happen right away.

The rest of the book discusses the signs and stages of pregnancy and how to prepare and support your partner and newborn before, during, and after pregnancy. Let's start at the beginning of the journey, which is recognizing the signs. We'll discuss this in the following chapter.

RECOGNIZE THE SIGNS

At the beginning of a pregnancy, most women display few to no symptoms, and some of them say that they don't even feel any differently. Suppose this happens to your partner, who is actually carrying a new life inside her body. In that case, you are most likely not to be able to tell what's going on... unless youdecide to take an active part and learn everything about the most common signs of pregnancy as well as what's normal and whatisn't in this very first stage.

It's more important than you think. Knowing and becoming involved in the pregnancy right from the start is not just a way of supporting your partner. Studies show men's involvement plays a huge role in decreasing maternal morbidity and mortality (Gize et al., 2019), so with your knowledge, you are also protecting the mother of your child. As you carefully go through this chapter, consider how the knowledge you get can be used either for reassuring your partner everything is okay whenever she gets anxious (something completely understandable) or, if necessary, to take her to the emergency room if that's the case.

A QUICK BIOLOGY CL ASS

We guys can generally get a woman pregnant at any time. However, the chances of pregnancy depend on several factors of the female body. Let's look at the cycles and learn how they can affect the chances of conceiving a baby. I know, you may have studied this subject before in high school, during sexual education classes. Still, if you were anything like me when I was a teen, you might not have paid enough attention (to be honest, by that time in my life becoming a dad was the least interesting thing about sex!).

What Is a Menstrual Cycle, and How Long Does It Last?

Women get their periods every month. This is the way their body repeatedly prepares for carrying a potential pregnancy. To count the days of the cycle, you start on the first day of bleeding up to the start of the following period. Some women have their period every 25 days, others every 30, and some have irregular cycles—meaning they don't always last the same number of days. The average length is around 28 days, the same as the moon cycle, but regular cycles between 21 and 41 days are also perfectly normal.

Ovulation occurs during the second half of the cycle. This is when the ovary releases an egg which your sperm can then fertilize. Some women don't necessarily ovulate every month despite having their period, which explains why it may take several cycles for a woman to get pregnant even if she's having regular sexual intercourse.

Something worth noticing is that many textbooks will place ovulation during day 14 of the cycle. Although this is true for the average 28-day cycle, it's not what happens in shorter or longer cycles. Ovulation occurs around 10 to 16 days before the next cycle. This means that if your partner gets her period every 34 days, she's likely to ovulate between days 18 and 24, later than what common calendars tell.

Tracking menstrual cycles is always a good idea, particularly when trying to conceive. It will allow you to calculate your fertility window and come in handy when pregnancy finally happens. Doctors calculate an estimated due date by counting from day 1 of the woman's last cycle.

Is Pregnancy Possible at Any Time During the Cycle?

There are no 100% safe sex days when it comes to pregnancy. It is possible—which is why you should *always* use some kind of birth control when you aren't trying to get pregnant— but it's unlikely to happen right before, during, or after the period. Women are fertile when ovulating, so it's important to calculate their particular fertility window according to their cycle. During those days, you have more chances to make a baby.

What About Irregular Menstrual Cycles?

Women who get irregular cycles or who skip monthly periods can have more difficulties getting pregnant since it isn't as easy to calculate their fertility windows. This may happen due to extreme weight gain or loss, stress, over-exercising, or some medical conditions we have already explored in Chapter 1. If your partner doesn't always get her period, or if you've been trying to conceive for a year without success, she should talk to her doctor.

However, it's worth noticing that many women with irregular periods will still be able to conceive. To maximize your chances of success, it's crucial to adopt a healthy lifestyle with a balanced diet, no alcohol or cigarettes, regular exercise, and plenty of rest.

Will Contraception Affect the Cycle?

Some birth control methods affect a woman's cycle, and you should take this into account if you want to have a baby. Of course, barrier methods such as the condom, sponge, diaphragm, or spermicide have no influence whatsoever on what happens with a woman's ovaries and eggs. On the other hand, if a woman is on the pill or takes contraceptive injections, her body needs a little adjustment period before "getting back on track" and returning to regular, fertile cycles.

How Long Does It Take to Get Pregnant After Stopping the Pill?

A woman who takes the pill gets monthly period-type bleeding, but she doesn't ovulate. While a pregnancy can happen right after coming off the pill, the best thing to do is to give the woman's body three months of adjustment before trying for a baby. This will allow her to get back to her natural periods. After this time, you may find out her cycles aren't as regular as expected—they are when a woman takes the pill—so if, after those three months, she's still irregular, it may be advisable to check with a doctor before trying.

Is Bleeding Normal When Pregnant?

Periods typically stop when pregnancy occurs. However, it's possible to experience some very light, painless bleeding (more of a spotting) called implantation bleeding, which takes place when a developing embryo plants itself in the wall of your partner's womb. Unlike real periods, this bleeding is usually pinkish or brown, not heavily red.

Some women bleed lightly before week 12 of their pregnancy. While most of the time it isn't anything serious, it's advisable to get her checked by her doctor, midwife, or early pregnancy unit just in case.

KNOW THE SIGNS

When my friends Daniel and Juliet finally relaxed about their infertility scare, it took little time for Juliet to get pregnant. As usual, she was looking forward to the most obvious sign: a missed period. However, even before that, she had the intuition something was going on. For a start, she was more tired and sleepy than usual, and getting out of bed in the morning took her forever.

Also, she suddenly found the smell of fresh coffee strangely repulsive—something she later realized was a common pregnancy-induced food aversion caused by the increased levels of the hormone estrogen.

Let's dig deeper into recognizing the early signs and symptoms before being sure about the pregnancy.

Early Symptoms

As in the story I told you, some women experience early signs and symptoms of pregnancy even when it's too early for a home test to confirm it. Keep in mind that none of these signs is a confirmation of pregnancy *per se*. However, if you are actively trying for a baby and your partner is experiencing some of them, chances are in your favor.

Skipping the Period

Bleeding is the way a woman's body gets rid of the thickening of the uterus lining that occurs every month as the body prepares for a possible pregnancy. When the egg doesn't get fertilized, the uterus sheds that lining, and it comes out of the body in the form of vaginal bleeding. But if fertilization occurs, the lining stays put, and the woman doesn't get her normal flow.

While a delayed or missed period is the most common early sign, it doesn't necessarily indicate pregnancy. We've seen some women have irregular periods, or they can skip them for multiple reasons other than pregnancy.

Food... or Not!

Just like Juliet experienced a sudden dislike for coffee, common food aversions include milk, tea, eggs, meat, onions, garlic, and spicy foods. Additionally, you've probably heard about "morning sickness," although it can happen at any time of the day. At the beginning of a pregnancy, hormonal changes can cause a woman to feel nauseous, vomit, or find specific smells or foods disgusting. Sometimes, they taste something metallic in their mouth even when they aren't eating anything. If your partner has food aversions or nausea, it's better to stay on the safe side and stick to bland foods such as chicken breast or crackers.

On the other hand, some women experience specific cravings during their pregnancy, a sudden desire for a particular item of food that they may or may not have liked before getting pregnant (my wife developed a passion for mushrooms!). In some cases, women crave non-food items, an eating disorder known as pica. Some women, during their pregnancy, feel the urge to feast on ice, soap, baby powder, or earth. Of course, unlike a normal food craving, you shouldn't indulge in pica when the item is potentially dangerous, and it's advisable to talk to your doctor about it, as it may point to a nutritional deficiency.

Changes in the Breasts

When a woman gets pregnant, her body experiences a sudden increase in hormones such as estrogen and progesterone, which are meant to support her developing baby. This may cause breast tenderness, swelling, or tingling even before the missing period tells the pregnancy.

Your partner's nipples also change. They may become sore, and the areolas (the areas around them) look darker. Although this usually happens gradually during pregnancy, some women can tell these signs early on.

Changes in Bathroom Breaks

After confirming the pregnancy, Juliet realized that for the past couple of days, she had been taking more frequent trips to the bathroom at work. Frequent urination happens because the amount of blood in the body increases during pregnancy, so the kidneys must work harder to filter it all.

On the other hand, many pregnant women experience bloating or constipation. If they appear as early as in the first trimester, these symptoms will likely last throughout the pregnancy.

Other Common Signs

Many women experience some of the following early pregnancy symptoms. Although isolated, none of them are indicators of pregnancy; if they happen all together or if you are actively trying to get pregnant, they may be noticeable before reading the result onthe pregnancy test:

- headaches

- mood swings

- dizziness

- nasal congestion

- fatigue

- lower abdominal pain

- higher basal body temperature

Confirming the Pregnancy

Since she and Daniel were actively trying to get pregnant, Juliet decided to take a pregnancy test even a few days before her bleeding was supposed to happen. It came out negative! Eventually, as days passed and Juliet still didn't get her period, she tooka second test. She carefully read the instructions, which stated towait at least two minutes before interpreting the result and taking the test with the first urine in the morning (somethingshe hadn't done the first time, as she admitted she was tooanxious). This time, the results were clear: A baby was on the way! Let's learn more about these types of tests and their accuracy.

Pregnancy tests work by detecting the presence of the hormone human chorionic gonadotropin (HCG). This hormone is produced by the placenta, something only pregnant women have. Tests can detect HGC either in urine or blood. Home pregnancy tests are basically little plastic sticks with a piece of reactive paper where the woman pees. You can buy them at any store without a prescription.

How do you read the results of a home pregnancy test? It depends on the brand of the test, but what you need to remember is that "positive" means pregnancy, and "negative" means no pregnancy. Some tests display two vertical lines for a positive, a plus sign, or even the word "pregnant." In any case, make sure you and your partner read the instructions that come with the test.

Home tests are easy to take and interpret, but are they accurate? When taken correctly, they offer a 99% accuracy. So, what happened to Juliet? Taking a home pregnancy test too early can cause a false negative when the traces of the hormone are yet too subtle to be detected, and some home tests are more sensitive than others. That's why it's advisable to wait at least until the first day of your partner's missing period to take one, and ideally a whole week. Other tips for better accuracy are using the first urine in the morning and not drinking excessive fluids, as they may affect the results.

Is there a way to get a false positive on a home test? Usually, when this happens, it's because the woman was pregnant then but lost the pregnancy shortly after the egg attached to the uterus wall. Additionally, some fertility drugs can cause a false positive onhome pregnancy tests (Cleveland Clinic, 2022a).

The blood tests are even more accurate than the pee tests, but your partner can't take them home, and they are more expensive. You can take her to the healthcare provider to have her blood tested. This is usually done to confirm the results of a test taken at homeor when a couple is going through fertility treatment and needs to know the results sooner than with a home pregnancy test. Blood tests are more accurate in the way they not only detect the presence of HCG but also its amount, which can help the doctor determine how advanced the pregnancy is.

POSSIBLE COMPLICATIONS

After getting a positive result on the test, your partner should start taking prenatal vitamins (if she isn't already) and quit drinking alcohol and smoking right away. It's particularly important to take folic acid—in supplements or her diet—to prevent neural tube defects in the developing baby. The pregnant woman also needs to schedule an appointment with her doctor, but there's no rush, as she doesn't need any medical studies during the first few weeks. However, certain symptoms may indicate something is wrong. Notice them and look for medical attention right away if they happen:

- **Bleeding:** It can be a sign of a miscarriage. Although some spotting is normal during the first weeks, you should consult your physician to see that nothing serious is going on.

- **Severe vomiting:** This is also known as hyperemesis gravidarum. If your partner experiences more than the occasional nausea, a doctor should treat her to prevent dehydration or malnutrition that could put both her and the baby in danger.

- **Pain:** While mild discomfort is expected, a sudden lower abdominal pain on a side may indicate an ectopic pregnancy, in which implantation occurs on the fallopian tube and can't go on. It must be treated as an emergency.

- **Miscarriage:** This is the loss of a pregnancy within the first half of it. It happens to 10%–20% of pregnancies, and 4 out of 5 miscarriages happen during the first trimester (Cleveland Clinic, 2022b).

Note that the first trimester is critical for the baby's development. Pregnancies at this stage may end in miscarriage, sometimes without the woman even noticing she was pregnant in the first place. This doesn't mean there's something wrong with your partner or that she can't successfully get pregnant and deliver a healthy baby in the following attempt.

KEY TAKEAWAYS

We've learned how to calculate a woman's fertility window from her menstrual cycle to maximize the chances of pregnancy. We've also learned about which symptoms are typical during the first stages of pregnancy and which others require immediate medical attention. In the following chapter, we'll get more details about what happens to your partner and future baby during the firsttrimester.

THE FIRST TRIMESTER

After receiving the confirmation of their pregnancy from Juliet's doctor, my friends were ecstatic: Their dream had come true, and they were going to have a baby! As days went by, Juliet wondered if it was normal to feel that... normal! Her initial symptoms had faded, she was still not showing, and although she was obviously missing her period, she couldn't help but wonder if everything was going okay. As weeks passed, some symptoms kicked in, and although they weren't pleasant, Juliet took them as a sign that the pregnancy was right on track.

At the same time, Daniel was overwhelmed with many questions: Would the stroller fit in the car's trunk? What was the best route to the hospital? By the way, did Juliet intend to have the baby in a hospital or at home? What was the best way to share the news with friends and family? How do you change a diaper? Fortunately, he and Juliet still had several months to prepare themselves.

If you are going through this stage of your partner's pregnancy, you are probably feeling equally confused. Don't worry! You aren't the only dad who feels unprepared. After all, a pregnancy lasts 40 weeks (around 9 months). You have time to educate yourself before you deal with an actual newborn. In this chapter, we will discover what happens to your partner and baby during the first trimester, what you should be aware of, and what you should do to support her.

WHAT HAPPENS IN...

Although most people speak about a pregnancy in "months," specialists prefer to approach it week by week, since the changes are so fast and spectacular. Let's see what's going on during this first crucial stage.

Weeks 1 to 4

The pregnancy journey begins when your partner isn't really pregnant. Can you believe it? This is because it's almost impossible for doctors to track down the moment when the actual conception took place. Ovulation dates are always estimated. Plus, the egg can wait around 24 hours to be fertilized by your sperm. So, if you had a romantic Valentine's night and she gets pregnant, that doesn't necessarily mean the baby was conceived on February 14th. To make things simpler, doctors refer to the day your partner had her last period as day 1 of pregnancy.

During weeks 1 and 2, there's no baby yet. Your partner's body is preparing for ovulation by thickening the uterus lining. She can already do some stuff to maximize your chances of success by taking folic acid, having a complete health check-up, and cutting down on cigarettes and alcohol. On the other hand, you can help make a baby by keeping your testicles cool. Instead of an electric blanket, snuggle with your partner. Turn off the heat and keep your laptop away from your lap! Heat slows down sperm production (Donaldson-Evans, 2023a).

Everything changes at some point in week 3. What could havebeen another menstrual cycle becomes officially a pregnancy when the sperm fertilizes the egg. What begins as a single, unique cell (called the zygote) starts its journey down the fallopian tube. In the meantime, it divides many times, creating a whole cluster of cells—about a hundred in just a couple of days! Your baby is on the way, although neither you nor your partner know it yet.

As the zygote becomes a blastocyst, cells divide into two groups: One develops into an embryo and the other into the placenta. Although you won't find out until the second trimester, your potential baby already has its own set of DNA, which means it's already either a boy or a girl, has encrypted the color of its future eyes and hair, and many other physical traits. In the meantime, it still looks like a microscopic ball of cells.

By week 4, the blastocyst reaches its destination, the uterine wall, where it implants, ready to develop and grow during the following 8 months. By the end of this week, your future baby will be as big as a poppy seed. During this time, around the embryo (what you'll call your future baby for the following weeks), a bag of water(called the amniotic sac) protects it while inside. The cells that will form the body begin to specialize. Some will create the digestive system; others, the heart; others, the hair and skin; and so on.

During these weeks, some women experience the first signs of pregnancy we discussed in Chapter 2, while others remain clueless. After all, they can feel cramps similar to those from their period or even spot their underwear with implantation bleeding. In any case, their bodies are beginning a massive transformation. Within 6 to 12 days after conception, the egg starts to release HGC, which means the traces of the hormone will soon be noticeable with a pregnancy test.

Weeks 5 to 9

During the second month of pregnancy, crucial changes occur in the embryo. At week 5, the placenta—an organ that connects the future baby to the uterine wall and provides your child-to-be with oxygen and nutrients—is beginning to develop. The mass of cells begins to take shape. Structures likethe neural tube (week 5), a pulsing heart (week 6), and tiny buds, which will become arms and legs, take shape at this early stage. Although still tiny, it grows a lot. In week 5, it's like anorange seed, but by week 8, it will already be as big as a raspberry, and doctors will be able to spot it on an ultrasound (andif you are expecting twins, you'll be shocked to see not one sacbut two!).

During these weeks, if you could see the embryo, you may notice that it looks like a tadpole with a tail that will eventually become its coccyx or tailbone. However, within weeks, you'll be able to recognize structures such as the eyes, ears, mouth, and other traits that resemble more of a baby's. By week 9, health providers no longer speak of your future baby as an embryo but as a fetus, with most of their major structures already formed and some spontaneous movement starting to occur (although, no, your partner can't feel any kicks yet!). It's time for rapid growth and development.

The hormonal torrent (mainly estrogen and progesterone) is responsible for your partner getting many annoying pregnancy symptoms during this first trimester—from nausea to dizziness, fatigue, swollen breasts, food aversion, and an increased sense of smell. She won't be "showing" yet, and some women even lose weight if they get morning sickness, but she will most likely start to feel pregnant.

Weeks 10 to 13

By the time you enter week 10 of the pregnancy, you are in the third month. Your baby is growing fast! By week 11, tiny toes and fingers separate from the hands and feet. By week 12, its digestive system begins to move into its abdomen. From the size of a prune to being as big as a lemon by week 13, the fetus already resembles a human baby... or a baby-ish alien, to be more accurate. Tiny teeth develop inside its gums, bones, and cartilage shape knees, ankles, and elbows, and its head takes up about half its size.

By the end of the first trimester, your partner's body has likely adjusted to all the hormonal rush, and her symptoms begin to decrease. By week 13, she's probably feeling a little bit more like herself, with fewer episodes of morning sickness, fatigue, and frequent need to pee, giving her a break. Some women start to show a little baby bump, which is actually her growing uterus.

Mother's Physical and Emotional Changes

As we have seen, the first trimester is a physical roller coaster for your partner. Although pregnancy is still invisible to others, many changes take place inside her body. This stage is commonly known for its discomfort: nausea, fatigue, painfully swollen breasts, an increment in vaginal discharge, dizziness... No wonder your partner has a low sex drive, right?

Plus, knowing that she'll become a mother causes differentemotions. Sure, she'll feel as happy as you since you were both trying to get pregnant. It's also normal for her to be scared. Justlike you, your partner wonders whether she'll be a good mom for the baby to come, but she's also afraid of her physical changes and delivery day approaching (although it's still far away). The first trimester is also a time of uncertainty. The risk of miscarriage isreal, and there's also doubt about whether the baby is healthy.Luckily, medical tests will provide comforting answers to help you both navigate the following months more easily.

Should you share the news with friends and family? The answer is entirely up to the two of you. Some couples decide to wait until the second trimester when the chances of miscarriage significantly decrease. But if you want to tell people, that's okay as well. Just make sure you are both on the same page when it comes to talking about the pregnancy.

WHAT YOU SHOULD KNOW...

Having a healthy pregnancy isn't only your partner's job. The more you take an active part of it, the better your chances of having a healthy baby within 9 months. Booking appointments and going to them together is also an excellent way for you to begin embracing your new role as a father and feeling empowered in it. Here's all you need to know about health professionals, medical tests, and prenatal appointments and how to accommodate your lifestyle to better suit your partner's needs during the firsttrimester of pregnancy.

Your Doctor

When it comes to pregnancy, there's no single type of doctor who can walk the journey with you, but your partner can make different choices. Be sure to explore different options for health providers and evaluate what's most important for you, depending on your particular needs and what your health insurance covers.

Obstetrician-Gynecologist (OB-GYN)

Commonly known as ob-gyns, obstetricians are medical doctors who specialize in women's health and pregnancy. After medical school, they receive a four-year residency program where they learn everything about reproduction, female health, pregnancy, and birth. Some of them specialize in high-risk pregnancies. This should be the best way to go if your partner has a preexisting medical condition, is expecting twins, or needs to have a cesarean delivery (C-section).

Certified Nurse Midwives

CNMs are professional nurses who receive training and are licensed specifically in obstetric and newborn care. Some women with low-risk pregnancies prefer to work alongside them because CNMs provide a much more family-centered approach and opt for birth plans as naturally as possible. They work alongside the ob-gyn, who can assist if complications occur at any point during pregnancy or delivery.

Family Practitioner

These doctors are trained to treat all sorts of health conditions of every family member, and some assist women during pregnancy and delivery. Your partner can have a family practitioner as the principal healthcare provider as long as they don't refer her to an ob-gyn—which they will do if there are complications during any stage of the pregnancy. One good thing about choosing a family doctor is that they can also care for your baby's health once they are born.

Perinatologist

If right from the start your pregnancy is considered high-risk, you may opt for a maternal-fetal medicine specialist known as a perinatologist. They may be the right choice if your partner is over 35, has diabetes, hypertension, a genetic disorder, or has had problems with a previous pregnancy. They are also the specialists you go to when you need to treat fertility problems.

Once you have asked for references from your friends and family and checked with your health insurance, you will probably have a narrowed list of providers. It's advisable to have interviews with several of them and trust your gut. The person who takes care of your partner during the pregnancy and delivers your baby should be someone you're comfortable with and who provides answers to all your questions and concerns.

Prenatal Appointments

You know your partner will need regular checkups with the health provider to ensure she goes through a healthy pregnancy and delivery. But you may be wondering what happens during those prenatal appointments. How often is she supposed to go? What can you expect from them?

The first prenatal appointment is the one that usually takes longer since the doctor or midwife not only performs a physical check-up—which includes taking blood and testing urine— but mostly talks to your partner and you about both your medical histories. The doctor checks your partner's weight, pulse, breathing, and blood pressure to make sure her health is in optimum condition or to treat whatever health issue theymay find. During this first visit, the doctor will indicate prenatal vitamins if she's not taking them and suggest some vaccines according to the ones your partner may or may not have.

In the following checkups, the doctor will measure your partner's belly, feel it to check the position of the fetus, indicate any tests or studies required, and answer any questions you may have.

Couples usually look forward to these prenatal appointments because they are the way to know everything's going great with their baby. They get to listen to their heartbeat and learn abouttheir growth. These appointments are the best moment to ask your health provider questions regarding pregnancy symptoms,changes in the woman's body, and how to prepare for delivery day.Make sure to ask the doctor about facilities in which they have admitting privileges so you can start taking tours.

How often does your partner need to get checked? This depends on two factors: the stage of her pregnancy and whether it's low-risk or high-risk. Any healthy pregnancy usually follows this schedule: one monthly prenatal visit until week 28, a visit every two weeks from week 28 to 36, and a weekly appointment for the last weeks of pregnancy (Kam, 2023). However, your doctor may suggest more frequent checkups if your partner is pregnant with twins or if they detect any risk factor before or during the pregnancy. Following up on the prenatal visit schedule is the best way to prevent complications ahead, such as preterm labor or delivery of a baby with low weight, so no matter how busy you both are, make sure you prioritize these checkups.

Tests and What They Do

During the first trimester, doctors suggest some tests to check on your partner and the baby. Your health provider may suggest more tests according to your partner's age, medical history, and whether she had complications during another pregnancy or delivered a baby with congenital disabilities. However, these tests aren't mandatory. You should decide as a couple if you have them done.

Your partner goes through a Pap smear and a pelvic exam to check the health of her cervical cells and detect any possible STD. She also has her blood tested to identify her blood type and Rh (rhesus) factor, detect possible anemia, find out she has immunity to rubella (German measles), and cross out other STDs. According to your specific racial, ethnic, and family background, some genetic counseling can also be suggested. Additionally, a urine test helps her health provider detect a possible kidney infection or diabetes and spot traces of protein that may indicate preeclampsia. This common pregnancy-induced disease should be checked, particularly after 20 weeks of pregnancy.

The first trimester is also when doctors suggest genetic screenings. This is a way a couple can find out their chances of delivering a baby with a chromosomal abnormality such as Down Syndromeor a congenital disability. However, it's worth noticing that mostof these tests don't provide 100% accuracy. According to the results, doctors may indicate further exams that are more invasive and aren't risk-free. With your partner, deciding whether you want them done or waiting until after delivery would be best. You must discuss all of your choices with your health provider.

First-trimester screening: This is a non-invasive test, meaning it doesn't involve risks to the developing fetus. It consists of a blood exam of the pregnant woman that measures two proteins and an ultrasound between weeks 11 and 14 that checks the skin behind the fetus' neck (called nuchal translucency). Afterward, doctors cross the results and come up with a statistic of the fetus having any abnormality. If the chances are low, you usually continue the pregnancy without further genetic tests. However, if doctors find any abnormality, they may suggest further studies.

Non-invasive prenatal testing (NIPT): This cell-free fetal DNA test tracks fetal DNA in a blood sample from the mother. It's non-invasive, and its accuracy for detecting Down syndrome and other chromosomal abnormalities is up to 99% (Johnson, 2023).

Chorionic villus sampling (CVS): A CVS is the most accurate test you can get during the first trimester. Doctors don't necessarily recommend it because it's an invasive procedure consisting of getting a tissue sample from the placenta with a tiny catheter through your partner's cervix or a needle through her abdomenand carries a 1% risk of subsequent miscarriage. However, it maybe advisable to have it done in specific cases, such as when you have a family history of specific diseases or if you get a positive result on previous non-invasive tests.

Diet and Lifestyle

A pregnant woman is feeding herself and developing her baby. That's why, during these months, it's more important than ever for your partner to follow a balanced diet. However, eating for two may be particularly challenging because of the first-trimester symptoms such as nausea, vomiting, food aversions, and fatigue. Fortunately, the baby is still too tiny to need extra food. Your partner can ensure she gets enough calories and nutrients by eating small amounts of food several times a day.

How can you help your partner fight nausea and food aversions? Offer her cold or room-temperature foods, which are generally better tolerated than hot servings. Liquids and soft-textured meals are also easier to pass. She should avoid spicy food if she suffers from heartburn. Additionally, drinking plenty of water during the day is the best way to ensure she stays hydrated. If she's not feeling particularly hungry, make sure whatever little food she gets is top quality and loaded with plenty of nutrients. During the first trimester, these are the most important:

- **Folic acid:** It's vital for preventing neural tube defects. Besides her prenatal vitamins, she gets folic acid from green leafy vegetables, cauliflower, beets, fruits (particularly oranges and strawberries), beans, nuts, and fortified cereals.

- **Protein:** It's necessary for building tissue. Offer her eggs, lean meat, chicken, and Greek yogurt.

- **Calcium:** It's vital for your baby's teeth and bones, and if your partner doesn't get the recommended daily 1,000 milligrams, she may lose it from her bones and have problems in the future. Ensure she eats three servings of dairy and plenty of leafy greens. Additionally, the doctor may recommend a supplement.

- **Iron:** It's vital for your partner's blood, and she can't satisfy her needs with food alone, so doctors usually recommend a supplement. In the meantime, it can be found in beef, chicken, tofu, eggs, and spinach. Whenever she takes her iron supplement, make sure she combines it with vitamin C for better absorption (pour her a glass of fresh-squeezed orange juice).

- **Potassium:** It's excellent for maintaining a proper fluid balance and preventing high blood pressure. Your partner gets it from foods like bananas, apricots, and avocados.

Now that you know which foods are best to include in your grocery list, let's see which foods pregnant women *shouldn't* eat. Raw and undercooked meat, fish, and eggs can lead to food poisoning and serious diseases such as listeriosis, salmonella, or toxoplasmosis. "These conditions can cause serious, life-threatening illnesses that could lead to severe congenital disabilities and even miscarriage" (Holland, 2023). The same applies to deli meat and unpasteurized dairy: No soft cheese, sushi, soft-served ice cream, or Peruvian ceviche for your partner! Every fruit and vegetable she eats must be washed carefully. Of course, she should also stay away from any kind of alcohol and limit her coffee intake to one or two cups.

Besides eating a healthy diet, the list of pregnancy recommendations includes exercising—following the routine if she already does or asking the doctor for a new workout plan— getting lots of sleep, and including a multivitamin even if she eats all her meals. Yoga routines are perfect for relaxing, and they provide light exercise, perfect for pregnant women. What about sex during the first trimester? With all the hormonal discomfort, some women experience a lull in their sex drive. However, as long as there isn't a complication, sex is allowed during pregnancy, and it's perfectly safe for your baby until the moment the water breaks (Holland, 2023).

WHAT YOU CAN DO...

During this first trimester, the best way to take care of your unborn baby is to be there for your partner. We've seen the mix of symptoms she might be experiencing! Let's see how you can better help her:

Support Your Partner

Going with your partner to prenatal appointments and helpingher follow a healthy diet and lifestyle aren't the only contributions you can make. You can also help her in these ways:

- **Quit smoking:** You're not the one carrying the baby, but second-hand smoking is nonetheless bad for pregnancy. Besides, if your partner needs to quit the habit herself, this is the best way to support her.

- **Let her sleep late:** She's experiencing fatigue and sleepiness. Let her rest an extra hour whenever possible. You can make breakfast before she gets out of bed.

- **Lift the heavy things:** Making efforts can hurt your partner's back. Make sure you do all the heavy lifting.

- **Take extra household duties:** Even if you divide the housework equally, allow her to rest. Additionally, being in charge of the cooking can save her from feeling disgusted by specific foods and smells.

- **Stay calm:** While your partner experiences symptoms and mood swings, remember they are normal and temporary.

- **Provide a listening ear:** Let your partner open up about her doubts and fears. You probably have yours, but you should talk about them with a friend with kids, your parents, or a counselor. Don't overwhelm her with more worries.

Prepare for the Next Few Weeks, Months, and Years

Another way to relieve some of your partner's burden is to be in charge of financial planning for pregnancy and after-baby. Having a child costs a lot of money! A 2017 report from the U.S. Department of Agriculture (USDA) states that the average family in theUnited States spends almost $300,000 raising a kid from birth to age 18—which doesn't include college tuition or accommodation(Batcha & Srinivasan, 2023).

You can tackle as many of the following as early as in the first trimester:

- Sign up for health insurance, both for your partner and the future baby. You should also consider investing in life insurance.

- If you already have insurance, update your beneficiaries to include your partner and future child.

- Check out the cost of prenatal services. If necessary,switch to a better plan as soon as possible.

- Find out about your workplace's parental leave policy. Look into special programs and apply if you need financialaid.

- Cut down on your credit card debt.

- Track your current spending and create a savings plan.

- Start coming out with a baby budget. Some ways to save are borrowing maternity clothes and buying second-handbaby gear.

KEY TAKEAWAYS

We've seen why the first trimester is usually the most challenging. The risks of the pregnancy at this stage are at their peak; everything is new, and your partner goes through a lot of discomfort. However, there's plenty you can do to support her. Fortunately, as weeks pass, most women feel relief from their symptoms. The second trimester is, for many, the best part of the pregnancy. Let's look at that in the following chapter.

THE SECOND TRIMESTER

After Daniel and Juliet's pregnancy reached the milestone of 14 weeks, and they were given the good news that their first-trimester screen was normal, they finally decided to share the news with their friends and family. I was among the guests at a fun dinner party they hosted. My friends suggested playing charades, but after a few minutes of them being silly together and laughing out loud, we all found out they were trying to convey a message: "Juliet is chubby," "Daniel is holding a watermelon!" we shouted, although we had pretty much figured it out. After they confirmed the news and showed us a picture of the sonogram, we clappedand cheered, and the party became even happier!

For Juliet and Daniel, and many other expecting couples, sharing the news brings significant improvement, as they get all sorts of social support for the rest of the pregnancy. Juliet's mom and sisters created a WhatsApp group to share tips, healthy recipes, and reminders for her to take her iron supplement. Daniel no longer felt so lost, as he could refer his doubts to his friends who were already dads. "Feeling well supported during pregnancy can offer a sense of connection and belonging, as well as emotional comfort and reassurance, which can help you manage any worries or concerns that may arise," explains psychologist and pregnant health support Dr. Lauren Rockliffe (2023).

Social support networks are even more important for single moms. Without social connection, they risk feeling isolated, anxious, or depressed, and they find it harder to go through the prenatal visit schedule and adopt a healthy lifestyle. Although Juliet and Daniel had each other, they found their social support improved their pregnancy journey in every sense. "Having people around you who have been through the same experience can also be helpful when trying to adjust to your changing body, as they can offer advice on how to deal with the physical and emotional changes" (Rockliffe, 2023).

Sharing the joy of their pregnancy is one of the reasons why the second trimester is the best stage for many couples. The woman experiences relief from the first trimester's most annoying symptoms as her body adjusts to the pregnancy. She enjoys showing off her growing belly and becomes more confident in her capability of carrying a healthy baby as the chances of miscarriage significantly decrease. For many couples, the second trimester is also the time to know about the sex of the baby, which is exciting as you get to imagine this new person that will change your life forever, think of a name, and dream of the approaching day when you will hold him or her in your loving arms. We'll see all about this second stage in this chapter.

WHAT HAPPENS IN...

Your future baby, now officially a fetus, already has most of its organs and body parts but still needs to grow exponentially to be able to survive outside the uterus. Here are the major changes the baby and the mother experience during the second trimester:

Weeks 14 to 17

By the time the fourth month of the pregnancy begins, the baby is moving constantly inside the uterus, although it's still too early for the mother to feel these movements. Baby's body grows from the size of a small orange to the size of a big onion, and it starts to get covered in a soft layer of hair (called lanugo), which protects it and helps maintain the right temperature. Their facial features are slowly moving into place. By week 15, the ears are positioned by the sides of the head, and the eyes are also migrating to their final position. By week 16, they are already sensitive to light. Babies in week 17 are very active, practicing breathing movements, sucking, swallowing, and holding their neck straighter than before. Soon, your partner will be able to feel them as a tiny fish swimming inside her.

For many women, this is the time when fatigue, morning sickness, and other unpleasant first-trimester symptoms finally vanish. Your partner will feel more energetic and enjoy walks—for example, when shopping for maternity clothes! But if she still looks pretty slim, don't worry. Not every woman shows a fully popped pregnant belly yet. However, even if she's feeling great, she still needsto take good care of herself. Her immune system relaxes during pregnancy, and she's more prone to getting sick. Make sure your partner gets the flu shot, and if she gets a little under the weather, don't hesitate to call the doctor. She can take many medicines which are compatible with the pregnancy, but she should only take them when prescribed.

The second trimester is usually easier than the first and the last one. However, believe your partner if she says she isn't feeling like herself. Some second-trimester typical symptoms include back pain, round ligament pain, a stuffy nose, heartburn, and indigestion. Discuss these symptoms at your following prenatal appointment, as most can be relieved. You can also suggest your partner schedule a dentist appointment. "Hormones can affect the gums, ligaments, and bones in your mouth, which in turn can slightly loosen the teeth, especially if you have more serious untreated conditions like gingivitis or periodontitis" (Donaldson-Evans, 2023b).

Weeks 18 to 22

The fifth month of pregnancy is an exciting time for many parents-to-be because they finally get to find out whether they are having a boy or a girl! By week 18, genitals become visible so doctors can tell you the result on your next ultrasound... unless your little one decides to play a little hide-and-seek! Doctors will also tell whether all the organs are developing appropriately. On the screen, you could also catch your baby yawning or hiccupping!

Between 18 and 22 weeks, most women begin to feel the baby's movements. First, it may seem like a little rumble inside the belly that could be mistaken for gas. But as days go by, the little kicks become more noticeable. When your baby isn't sleeping, they practice grabbing, tasting what your partner feasts on, and listening to your voice with their developing sense of hearing. It's such an exciting time!

Around halfway through the pregnancy, your baby is still quite tiny. By week 20, they weigh just 10 ounces, but don't worry—they are growing fast! By week 22, most babies break the 1-pound mark. Their skin is covered in a cheesy varnish called vernix caseosa that protects it from the surrounding amniotic fluid. Some babies are born covered in that substance, which isn't appealing, but it's normal and healthy.

Your partner is probably showing a noticeable pregnant belly as her uterus grows. It has become so large that it's starting to shift the center of gravity, which may cause back pain as it pulls your partner's lower back forward. At the same time, the growing uterus pulls up the stomach, so heartburn and indigestion become more frequent. Remind your partner to eat her food slowly and sit down while you do the dishes. She should also increase her fiber intake to prevent constipation since digestion becomes slower. She should take things easy, as she's probably not sleeping peacefully every night. Leg cramps become annoying, and the pain from them can wake her up.

Her appetite is probably at its best. The doctor will control her weight gain to make sure it's within a normal range. Her stomach isn't the only growing body part; her feet sometimes expand into a new shoe size! She may like some changes better than others—but for the love of God, you always tell her she looks glowing and beautiful, no matter what the scale says. Between us dads, if you are caring and romantic, she'll show you her appreciation! This second trimester may be a honeymoon for you since many women recover their sex drive, and the baby belly still allows most of the sex positions. Enjoy being together! Once the baby is born, intimacy will have to wait.

Weeks 23 to 27

As the pregnancy approaches the end of the second trimester, your baby prepares for a significant growth spurt, in which they'll double their size in about a month. At the same time, your partner may experience considerable weight gain to support all this development. By week 23, your baby's skin is transparent and saggy, but soon, fat tissue will deposit inside their body to give them that lovely chubby newborn appearance they'll have three months later when they are finally born. By week 24, their facial features are already more defined—from this time onward, you could have a hint on who your baby resembles by having a 4D or 5D sonogram. By week 26, the baby opens their eyes. If you shine a flashlight in your partner's belly, you can sense some response fromthe inside!

During weeks 25 to 27, your baby's lungs quickly develop to allow them to breathe once they get outside the uterus. In fact, if, for some reason, a baby was born this early during pregnancy, they have a slight chance of surviving, although it would take a lot of time in the neonatal intensive care unit (NICU).

Just as your unborn baby experiences many changes this month so does your partner. She's probably gaining weight, which may cause her skin to stretch, creating itchiness and possibly some stretch marks. She can prevent some of them by applying moisturizer.And since we are talking about her skin, other changes due to pregnancy are the dark line that runs through her belly (from the belly button to the pubic area), known as the linea nigra. She should also protect herself from sunlight, as some women tend to get spots on their faces, and sunburn would make them permanent.

"Mommy brain" is a real thing! Not getting enough sleep, being anxious about the delivery date approaching, and physical changes can cause your partner to become more distracted and clumsy. Go easy on her! Other symptoms she can experience are red, itchy palms, swelling of her feet and legs (and other body parts as well! Some pregnant women deal with the discomfort of hemorrhoids), or changes in her vision. Although most of these symptoms are compatible with a healthy, normal pregnancy, make sure to discuss them with the health care provider during the prenatal appointments.

Mother's Physical and Emotional Changes

Most women describe the second trimester as the best part of their pregnancy. Their bodies are already adjusting to hormonal changes—though this doesn't mean they don't experience some uncomfortable symptoms—and since they share the news and begin to show, they usually receive sympathy and support from their friends, family, and coworkers.

As the pregnancy continues to develop, it gets easier to imagine the baby you will have in a few months (although, believe me, babies are never exactly as you imagined them; your child will always surprise you!). It's a great time to talk about baby namesand to have long talks about parenting styles, education, and how the two of you will team up to give this child a great family environment.

While your partner is more energetic and in a better mood than the previous trimester, keep pampering her and make sure she doesn't take up additional efforts. If she's feeling fine, take advantage of these weeks and go out just the two of you! Go see a movie, eat at her favorite restaurant, or take a brief "babymoon" somewhere romantic. Pretty soon, date nights are going to become way more complicated!

WHAT YOU SHOULD KNOW...

During the second trimester, the doctor will continue to check your partner's health and perform a series of tests. These tests aren't just for confirming that all is well with your baby but also to detect and prevent possible health conditions that can happen in the second part of the pregnancy, such as gestational diabetes or high blood pressure. This is also the stage to start considering the birth plan. Let's have a closer look at what it means.

Birth Plan

Perhaps you're wondering what exactly a birth plan is. As the name indicates, it's a written outline where the pregnant woman (and her partner) list down her choices when it comes to labor day regarding the details of the type of birth she looks forward to, the procedures she would like to have done (if any), and overall her preferences for before, during, and after childbirth. Coming up with a birth plan is, for many couples, a way to empower themselves before the delivery day and to find out about the many choices available—as long as the pregnancy and delivery are without complications.

While it isn't mandatory to come up with a birth plan, it's always a good idea to discuss the details with your doctor, and it's advisable to have the plan written if several professionals are attending the birth. You could print copies of the birth plan to ensure they align with your partner's desires. She may leave some details blank if she's uncertain. For example, she may not be sure how she feels about being given an epidural. Maybe she can control the pain with relaxation and breathing techniques, but she wants to havethe choice in case it becomes unbearable. That's also okay!

Just keep in mind that no birth plan is written in stone. Your partner may change her mind regarding specific preferences—and she should be listened to! Besides, doctors may indicate certain procedures if any complication arises during later pregnancy stages or labor. The birth plan displays the best-case scenario, but the hospital where you decide to give birth may allow or denysome of your preferences. Jennifer Geddes, from *What to Expect*, puts it this way: "The most important part of a good birth plan is flexibility. Childbirth is unpredictable. The best-laid plans don't always go, well, according to plan" (2021).

Tests and What They Do

If your partner stays healthy and no unexpected complications appear during the second trimester, her doctor will still want to check on her every month. Additionally, during this stage, the following tests will be suggested:

- **Routine tests:** The doctor will check your partner's weight and blood pressure and periodically test her urine, looking for protein, sugar, or any kind of infection. Plus, the height of the uterus (or fundal height) is measured to confirm the baby's growth, and the baby's heart can be heard with a hand-held ultrasound device.

- **Midtrimester ultrasound (the 18 to 20-week scan):** Thisis an exciting ultrasound because, for many couples, it's when they learn about the sex of the baby they're expecting. However, you should keep in mind it's a major medical study done for many reasons, so you shouldn't skip it even if you want to keep the sex a surprise until birth. Doctors perform the second-trimester sonogram toconfirm the due date, examine the anatomy of the fetus and its blood flow patterns, check the amount of amnioticfluid, observe fetal activity and behavior, measure the length of your partner's cervix, monitor fetal growth, and see where the placenta is located.

- **Glucose screening:** Even healthy women have the chance of developing diabetes during their pregnancy; that's why doctors recommend this one-hour glucose tolerance exam. Your partner will drink a sugar solution and get her blood tested an hour afterward. Further exams may be indicatedif any abnormal blood sugar level appears. It's worth noticing that gestational diabetes can be treated with diet,exercise, and medication, and it usually goes away shortly after delivery.

- **Multiple marker tests/AFP4 screen/quad screen:** It's another blood test that tracks certain blood substances that indicate the risk—not the certainty—of chromosomic abnormalities. If the test comes out positive, doctors may suggest the following:

- **Amniocentesis:** It consists of the analysis of amniotic fluid the doctor extracts by inserting a needle through the abdomen into the amniotic sac. By studying the fetal cells contained in the fluid, doctors can tell almost for sure if the fetus has any genetic disorder or a neural tube defect. This test isn't performed in every pregnancy, only if some abnormalities were found on the NIPT in the first trimester, on the AFP in the second trimester, or if your partner has higher chances of carrying a baby with a congenital disability or a chromosomic disease. It's usually done between weeks 15 and 20, and while doctors may suggest it, it's up to you as a couple to discuss its pros and cons because it's invasive and carries a small risk of losing the pregnancy. For example, if you decide you'll still carry on with the pregnancy if the fetus is at risk of having Down Syndrome, you may decide against amniocentesis.

WHAT YOU CAN DO...

As the pregnancy develops, your role continues to be important! Besides discussing with your partner the pros and cons of medical tests and coming up with a birth plan, there are many ways you can support her during this stage.

Support Your Partner

Here's what your partner would love you to do:

- **Give her a massage:** The ligaments in her body naturally become softer. If your partner complains about lower back pain, a gentle massage could help her feel better. Remind her to put her feet up to relieve swollen ankles. "A massage can melt away pregnancy aches and pains. It may also help you relax and sleep better" (Pathak, 2021).

- **Relieve her headaches:** Many women experience migraine or headaches during pregnancy. Give her paracetamol, which is perfectly safe, and try to relieve any stress in her daily routine.

- **Tell her she looks amazing:** Your partner may be concerned about all her physical changes during this stage. Be reassuring and supportive about her appearance.

- **Have sex with her:** Many women feel friskier during the second trimester! Don't be afraid to hurt your partner or the baby. Unless your doctor advises against it, sex during pregnancy is safe and pleasurable for both of you. As the belly grows, make sure your partner is comfortable. "If sex is uncomfortable right now, try new positions. Lie on your side or try getting on your hands and knees to accommodate your growing belly" (Pathak, 2021).

- **Research childbirth classes:** Soon, you two will attend preparation for labor. Find out what your health provider offers and sign up. You can also take parenting or first-aid classes to feel better prepared for the baby's arrival.

- **Connect with your baby:** You can achieve this by talking or singing to them. By this stage, their hearing is already developing, which can help your baby get used to your voice. Soon, you'll be able to feel their movements whenplacing a hand on the bump.

- **Paint the nursery:** Besides doing any heavy lifting, a chore you should definitely take on is decorating your baby's future room. Your partner shouldn't inhale any paint fumes or wallpaper glue.

- **Visit the hospital:** This is already a good time to explore the facilities of the place where you plan to have the baby. In some hospitals, you can already pre-register.

Baby's Sex and Names

When it comes to the baby's sex, which one is better? To find out or to wait? Some couples can't wait for the doctor to tell them whether the baby is a boy or a girl, while others decide to keep the secret until delivery. There's no right answer, and you and your partner must decide for yourselves. Keep in mind the following:

If You Decide to Know

Finding out alleviates some of the pregnant couple's anxiety. Many find they can better relate to the baby once they start picturing him or her according to the sex and giving the baby a name. Even if they expected the opposite, they still have many months to adjust their expectations. Plus, they get to decorate the nursery and get baby's clothing according to traditional styles for boys or girls. Finally, the fun of throwing a gender-reveal party with all blue or pink is yet another advantage.

It's not all pros, though. For a start, tests could be wrong, and you'll end up dressing a boy all in pink or a girl all in blue if they made a mistake, especially when friends and family usually put a lot of emphasis on traditional gender colors when buying gifts for the baby. Some couples believe it's better not to put so much emphasis on a child's sex, especially since gender roles depend on manyother factors rather than biology. "While sex can be determined before birth, a person's gender is not typically chosen until childhood, adolescence, or beyond" (Terreri, 2017).

If You Keep Baby's Sex a Secret

Some couples love the element of surprise! They choose two or more names for the baby and decorate the nursery in neutral tones such as green or yellow. They refrain from assigning their unborn baby stereotypical traits regarding their sex and ask their friends and family for gender-neutral clothes. There's no chance of disappointment when you find out if you are already holding a newborn.

The cons of not knowing are mainly dealing with societal pressures. Your friends and family may drive you crazy, and their disappointment of not knowing may be hard to deal with.

What if your partner wants to keep the secret, but you desperately need to know, or the other way around? While some people may be okay with one of them talking to the doctor in private andkeeping the news for themselves, it's probably better to communicate honestly and reach for a joint decision. Accidentally spillingthe beans may be a source of conflict within the couple.

Tips for Choosing Names

Maybe you've decided on your baby's name way before trying to get pregnant. Or perhaps now your baby is on the way, you feel overwhelmed with name suggestions from everyone around you! How can you pick the perfect name for your baby? Here are some suggestions:

- **Sources of inspiration:** You may find a great name inspired by a location, someone from pop culture, or your cultural inheritance. Of course, if you are more comfortable sticking to a religious name or carrying on a family tradition, that's great, too!

- **Alphabetical lists:** How about choosing the initials before the name? From there, you can check out alphabetical lists online and find the best name for a boy or a girl that better goes with the last name(s) the baby will carry.

- **Reasons for having a middle name:** While many people don't find any practical use in having a middle name, it can come in handy for "hiding" that traditional family name you don't adore, for allowing yourselves to be playful— John Legolas Smith? Why not? Or for giving your child a chance in the future in case they don't share your preference for their first name.

- **Can you choose a last name?** Depending on where your baby is born, you may or may not choose the baby's last name. In some states or countries, giving the child their father's last name is mandatory if it's known. Other people choose to use both the dad's and the mom's last names, whether hyphenating them or combining them into a new last name (Murray, 2023).

- **Watch out for nicknames and difficult spellings:** When considering names, check out potential nicknames and seeif they match both the middle and the last names and don'tsound funny. Regarding spelling, you need to find a balance between giving your child a unique name and creating a future nightmare at school when their teachers get it wrong every single time.

INTERACTIVE ELEMENT: COME UP WITH THE RIGHT BIRTH PL AN

If you and your partner haven't created a birth plan yet, here are some questions you should ask yourselves to include in the outline. Afterward, you can either have it written or simply discuss the details with your health provider. Remember, any birth plan is only a guideline based on your partner's preferences, but the ultimate goal is to deliver the baby in the safest way possible for both mother and child.

- If given the choice, which type of childbirth would you prefer?

- Where do you want to give birth? At home or in a hospital facility?

- Would you like to be able to move around, drink fluids, and play music during labor?

- How would you like to control the pain? Would you like to be given anesthesia?

- Who should be allowed to be in your room during labor?

- Which elements would you like to try during labor? (a birthing ball, birthing chair, bathtub, etc.)

- Do you have a birthing position of preference?

- Do you agree with using a catheter or an enema?

- Are you okay with having permanent fetal monitoring/rupture of the membranes/an episiotomy?

- Do you plan to store/donate umbilical cord blood?

- Do you allow pictures/videos during delivery? Who should take them?

- Who is going to hold the baby/cut the umbilical cord/go with the baby when they have the medical procedures done?

- If your baby is a boy, will you have him circumcised?

- Do you plan to breastfeed or bottle-feed?

- Would you rather have the baby stay in your room or a nursery if available?

KEY TAKEAWAYS

We've learned about what to expect during the second trimester. In addition to following up on prenatal visits, remember the importance of building a support group with your friends and family, coming up with baby names, and coming up with a birth plan. In the following chapter, we'll discuss the third trimester.

HELP FUTURE DADS NAVIGATE THE JOURNEY

Embrace the Gift of Guidance

"The best way to find yourself is to lose yourself in the service of others."

— MAHATMA GANDHI

Those who share wisdom with no expectation of reward often find greater fulfillment and joy in life. So, why not give it a shot?

To kickstart that journey, let me pose a question...

Would you lend a hand to someone you've never met, even if you never received recognition for it?

Who might this person be, you wonder? They're akin to you. Or, at least, to the version of you from yesteryears. Eager but uncertain, craving to make a difference, yet unsure where to turn.

My aim? To simplify the journey of impending fatherhood for dads everywhere. Every effort I exert stems from this purpose. And, the only way for me to achieve it is by reaching... well...everyone.

This is where you can play a pivotal role. As it turns out, many individuals do judge a book by its cover (and its reviews). So, here's my humble request on behalf of a struggling new dad you've yet to meet:

Would you kindly lend your voice by leaving a review for this book?

Simply scan the QR code below to leave your review:

Your contribution demands no monetary investment and merely a fraction of your time, yet it holds the potential to forever alter the trajectory of a fellow father's life. Your review might just...

Provide invaluable guidance during pregnancy, foster confidence, and strengthen familial bonds to positively impact a new dad's life.

To Leave A Review Go To:

Amazon.com

-Or Scan Below –

THE THIRD TRIMESTER

As months went by and delivery day was approaching, Julietand Daniel were very active decorating the nursery in shades of green—they chose not to find out about the baby's sex—purchasing baby gear (a stroller, crib, car seat, and other stuff theycouldn't borrow), and following up with prenatal appointmentsand tests. It wasn't until week 34 that they started their childbirth classes, and that's because Juliet's ob-gyn told them to.

Daniel told me later that he felt a bit useless at first, realizing that everything about the birthing process was up to Juliet and Juliet alone. However, one good thing about attending the course was that he learned all about warning signs and how to tell if the baby was about to arrive. This came in handy when, one morning during breakfast, early in week 38, Juliet experienced a suddenback pain. Despite her complaints, Daniel rushed to get her to the hospital. Fortunately, they had packed the hospital bag a few nights before!

As the due date approaches, it's more important than ever to be prepared for the symptoms and be able to tell what's normal and what isn't. Your partner is likely to be uncomfortable in this last stage, and it's part of your duty to help her feel empowered and reassured about what's going to happen. Women are prepared to carry and deliver babies. She's got this, and you've got this, too! Let's find out what happens during the third trimester, the laststage of pregnancy.

WHAT HAPPENS IN…

By the time the pregnancy enters the third trimester, if you could peek at the fetus, you'd discover it already resembles a tiny baby with all its body parts and features. However, it's not yet time to be born; it still needs to grow and gain strength.

Weeks 28 to 32

During the seventh month of pregnancy, your baby spends a lot of time sleeping and dreaming—something specialists know because fetuses this age experience rapid eye movement (or REM), the stage of sleep when dreams happen. Their eyes remain closed most of the time, but they can blink them, and they already have eyelashes. Although your partner should feel them move several times a day, the baby isn't doing those spectacular acrobatics as before since the uterus is more cramped—and it's about to get even more so! By week 29, the baby's length is close to its birth size, but it still needs to double its weight. By the time the pregnancy reaches week 32, the baby will likely settle in the head-down position.

Your baby's brain, in particular, experiences huge changes during these weeks. Not only does it get bigger, but it also gets more wrinkled as it allows more room for brain tissue. The connections between brain cells are fundamental for supporting your baby once they are born, but even now, they allow your child to process information from their developing five senses.

Your partner is becoming a bit more uncomfortable as her belly grows, and she may experience annoying symptoms such as sciatica (tingling leg pain) and swollen blood vessels. She might not be able to sleep comfortably anymore as the baby is probably more active at nighttime, and the skin over her belly feels tight and itchy. Some of the symptoms of early pregnancy come back, such as frequent urination and heartburn, although now it's not because of the hormones but due to the pressure of the uterus on the other organs. This can also cause her to become short of breath, something that will improve once the baby's head drops down into her pelvis as they prepare for birth.

Weeks 33 to 37

As the middle of the trimester approaches, your baby has reached the length they'll measure once they are born, but by week 33, they are still putting on half a pound weekly. Although premature babies born during the eighth month of pregnancy have good chances of developing properly without any consequences, they should stay inside as long as possible, at least until week 37, when they are considered full-term babies.

During these weeks, besides gaining weight, your baby is developing their immune system, shedding the waxy coat that kept them protected the past months, growing their fingernails, and accumulating body fat and gray matter. All they have to do now is to practice for their life outside the uterus. They inhale and exhale amniotic fluid, swallow it, and suck their thumb.

Your partner is likely experiencing periodical Braxton-Hicks contractions, which are "practice" contractions. Unlike the real ones, they aren't painful and usually disappear when she changes her position. During birth classes, you will learn how to tell if it'stime to go to the hospital or if you can still wait at home. By the time the baby drops, she'll start waddling and possibly experiencing some pelvic discomfort because of the pressure of the baby's head.

Weeks 38 to 42

It's the final countdown! By week 39, your baby is fully developed and could be born any time now. During the following days, they are shedding the lanugo, their skin has gained a pinkish to white appearance (the pigmentation occurs shortly after birth), and their eyes have turned the color they'll have at birth—although this may not be the permanent shade, as they may keep changing until baby's first birthday. By week 40, the ninth month of pregnancy is complete, although the two of you may feel it has lasted several years.

Besides anxiety, fear of labor, insomnia, and a strong nesting instinct, your partner may experience leaky breasts. They produce colostrum, which will be your baby's first food. She may also lose her mucus plug, a yellow or brownish discharge of a substance that has been keeping her cervix close but not anymore for obvious reasons. And no, it's not a sign that delivery is immediate, as it can be lost weeks prior!

What happens if the due date passes? Well, nothing! About 1 in 3 pregnancies hit the 41-week mark (Donaldson-Evans, 2023c). Babies aren't considered overdue until week 42 because their late check-up is probably a miscalculation of the original due date. However, if you reach this point, after careful monitoring, the baby's doctor will induce labor.

Mother's Physical and Emotional Changes

The last trimester of pregnancy is challenging for your partner. As the baby gains weight, so does she, and carrying such a big belly makes it hard for her to engage in simple daily tasks, such as riding public transportation, doing groceries, or even tying her shoelaces! She's not getting a good night's sleep (and she's not likely to get one any time soon!), and labor approaching can make her anxious.

With all these changes, she may not recognize herself in the mirror. Remind her that the transformation she's going through is part of the miracle of carrying a new life inside her, and tell her she glows. If she gives you a look of disbelief, praise her hair. Hormones are responsible for it growing longer, stronger, and falling much less, so it's a positive side effect of pregnancy!

You will insist on lifting heavy stuff and telling her to get some rest, but if she's often seen around the house emptying cupboards or vacuuming the floors, that's not because she lost it. It's a natural consequence of pregnancy called the nesting instinct. While it can be useful to finish setting up the nursery or pre-washing all those lovely baby clothes she got at her baby shower, remind her not to overdo it. She needs to save some energy for the big day!

WHAT YOU SHOULD KNOW...

With the delivery day approaching, you and your partner are up to more frequent checkups and medical tests. Besides, this is an excellent time to interview pediatricians for your baby.

Your Baby's Doctor

Three months before the due date is a great time to start searching for a pediatrician for your child. This isn't a matter to be taken lightly, as their doctor will be the most important person to look after your child's health for their entire childhood and adolescence. Not only do they see children when they are sick, but they also monitor their growth and development, offer answers regarding sleep and feeding, and perform immunizations.

You should fully trust your baby's doctor and feel secure with their advice and guidance. Alanna Nuñez, from *What to Expect*, believes a pediatrician is more than your baby's doctor because even when they are there to prescribe cough medicine or flu shots, they "will also be there to answer your questions about postpartum depression or anxiety and assure you on the bad days that you're actually doing a good job at this whole parenting-a-new-human-being- thing" (Nuñez, 2022). Therefore, you need to find someone who aligns with your family's values. If you haven't met them yet, youare likely to have more than one interview until you find the righthealth professional for your family.

To start your search, you can ask for recommendations from your friends and family and then check with your insurance to see if any of those doctors are in your plan. Additionally, you can read online reviews of professionals in your area. You can opt for a pediatrician or a family physician, who treats patients of all ages. Of course, whoever you choose, you need to make sure they are board-certified, meaning they are fully qualified to treat your baby.

How can you decide between a couple (or several) of highly qualified doctors? How can you tell who the right professional is foryou and your baby? Here are some tips:

- **Proximity:** You'll need to check up on your baby several times, especially during the first year, as doctors monitor their growth. If you have to drive an hour to the doctor's office, it will become an inconvenience, even if you havean emergency room nearby.

- **Availability:** When is the doctor available? Are they part of a team, and could other doctors or nurses check on your baby if they were temporarily unavailable? Do they accept video calls? Do they offer schedules on the weekends and evenings? Who should you call when the doctor is on vacation? How should you handle emergencies?

- **Costs:** How much will you pay after each visit? Does your insurance cover at least part of it? Must you pay in full each time, or can you pay over time if necessary?

- **Values:** Make sure your doctor's views align with yours regarding breastfeeding or bottle-feeding, co-sleeping, vaccines, antibiotics, potty training, circumcision, and any other aspect you and your partner find important.

- **Environment:** During your interview, check the waiting room. Is it child-friendly? How long do the other families have to wait? Is the office clean and tidy?

- **Treatment:** How do you feel during the interview? Does the doctor take the time to answer all of your questions, or do they seem in a rush? Are they clear and respectful, or do they use a condescending tone? The right professional will feel right. More than their credentials, you need to listen to your gut!

Prenatal Appointments, Tests, and What They Do

Before taking your baby to the pediatrician, your partner mustbring them into the world! During this last stage of pregnancy,she's expected to attend more frequent prenatal appointments. By the time she gets to week 28, the doctor will ask her to come every two weeks, and as the due date approaches, from week 36 onwards, every week. While it may sound like you'll spend a lot of time around the doctor's office, these close checkups usually reassure many expecting couples.

During the appointments, the now usual controls take place. The doctor will measure your partner's weight and blood pressure, as well as the size of her belly, and listen to the baby's heartbeat. Sometimes, they request a urine sample or indicate further studies, especially if yours is a high-risk pregnancy. For example, if your partner develops common pregnancy-related diseases such as preeclampsia or gestational diabetes, a third-trimester sonogram will be necessary to make sure the baby's growth and development are adequate. Additionally, if a previous ultrasound showed placenta previa (when the placenta partially or totally covers the cervix), doctors need to check whether the problem has been resolved or if it's necessary to program a C-section.

If your partner tests Rh-negative, she will receive an injection of Rh immune globulin that prevents her body from producing antibodies, something that could be bad news if your baby is Rh-positive.

Between 35 and 37 weeks, there's a painless yet uncomfortable test of group B strep. Your partner needs to have her anus and vagina swabbed to check for a common infection. If the results are positive, she is treated with antibiotics to prevent the baby being infected during labor.

Once your partner is past her due date, doctors may suggest a cervical check to see if it's softening, which could indicate labor is approaching. The baby's heartbeat and fetal activity are also monitored closely to ensure the pregnancy can continue until labor begins naturally. This can be done through a nonstress test (NST) or—less likely—a contraction stress test (CST) to see if the baby responds accordingly to stimulation.

Of course, prenatal appointments are the best place to talk about your partner's symptoms and ask any necessary questions you may have now that the final day is approaching. However, certain symptoms require you to call the doctor right away. These include:

- bleeding

- increased vaginal discharge that smells

- fever

- pain when she pees

- intense headache or blind spots in her eyesight

- sudden swelling or weight gain

- trouble breathing

- regular, painful contractions

- the baby isn't moving as often

- her water breaks

Antenatal Classes

Although you'll only learn to be a father by experience, it's a good idea to take some classes to feel empowered and help you get ready for what's ahead: mostly labor, birth, feeding a baby, and taking care of them during the first few months. These classes are known as antenatal classes, labor classes, or birthing classes, and both pregnant women and their partners may find it helpful to take them.

Antenatal classes usually take about eight hours to cover all the important topics. Since they revolve around the busy schedule of expecting couples, you take the course over several weeks. Therefore, it's a good idea to sign up for it when you enter the third trimester, around week 28 (or even earlier if you're expecting twins!). You can ask your partner's doctor or health provider for recommendations. You should also check with your health insurance company to see if they cover the cost of the class. Sometimes, you can find these classes in hospitals, charities, or private practices. However, the person who imparts them doesn't need to be a doctor. Doulas can teach private antenatal classes as well.

Which topics are covered in these classes? Here are some for you to get an idea:

- how to follow a healthy diet and lifestyle during pregnancy

- exercises for your partner on the last stage of the trimester

- what to expect during labor and birth

- relaxation techniques for natural birthing and pain relief information about the different possible interventions in childbirth, including what happens during a C-section

- when to go to the hospital

- how to take care of a newborn

- tips for breastfeeding

- what to expect for postpartum, including warning signs

- feelings and emotions before, during, and after childbirth

There's not a single type of antenatal class. You may find the traditional course available together with other options, such as

Lamaze, hypnobirthing, antenatal yoga or Pilates, or active birth, so make sure you explore different choices with your partner and find the one that better suits you. Some of them provide a general overview of all the aforementioned topics, while others are centered on something more specific, such as active movement during labor or breathing techniques to control pain without drugs.

Other than finding answers to your most common questions, these classes provide an opportunity to meet other expecting couples, which can be great for expanding your support group. "Friends made at antenatal classes often meet with each other through the first few months with their new baby and can be agreat source of support for each other" (*Antenatal Classes*, n.d.).

Hospital Bag

As your due date approaches, you need to make sure your partner has everything she needs for when the time comes to go to the hospital. Some women prepare the bag as early as week 33, while others decide to wait, but it's always better not to wait until the last minute. Remind your partner to have the hospital bag all packed by week 38 since the baby could be born any day then, and you don't want to rush things.

The length of the hospital stay depends on whether your partner has a vaginal delivery or a C-section. In the first case, she'll usually get admitted for two days, and in the second, maybe three or four.

What should you pack? While it's always a good idea to check with her doctor or the facility where she's going to have the baby which items she's requested to bring along, here is a checklist of the essentials:

For the Mom-To-Be

- **Documents:** Bring a photo ID or driver's license, insurance info, hospital paperwork, and one or morecopies of the birth plan you created.

- **Clothes:** Pack pajamas, warm socks, a comfy robe or a sweater, maternity bras, underwear that can fit big pads,and loose clothes for going back home.

- **Toiletries:** While the hospital will probably provide essential items such as maxi pads, soap, and shampoo, she may want to pack her own. Include a hairbrush or a comb, deodorant, toothbrush and toothpaste, lotion, lip balm, and nursing pads. If she's receiving visits, she may want tohave some makeup.

- **Personal items:** Bring her cell phone and charger, glasses or contact lenses, headbands, clips, or scrunchy, music and headphones, snacks for eating after labor, and some diversions for long labor, such as magazines, video games, or a fun book.

For the Baby

While the hospital usually provides everything the baby needs during their stay (including clothes, diapers, and wipes), you must remember the following essentials:

- **Infant car seat:** Have this device properly installed.

- **Clothes for coming back home:** Bring a onesie, socks, a hat, and extra layers of clothing depending on the weather—but don't overdress the baby! If they are born in the summer and it's 87 °F out there, they don't need a tiny jacket!

- **Pediatrician information:** It's a good idea to include their contact numbers and information for the hospital nurses.

- **Bottles:** If you plan to bottle-feed, make sure you include them in the hospital bag as well.

For You

- **Clothes:** Think as if you were taking a short trip! Take your pajamas, a T-shirt, extra socks, and underwear.

- **Toiletries:** Bring your shampoo, deodorant, toothbrush, toothpaste, contact lenses and solution, etc.

- **Snacks:** Bring a selection of snacks, reusable bottles, and lots of change for the hospital vending machines.

- **Entertainment:** Plan music, light reading material, your laptop, a deck of cards, and whatever items help you make the waiting hours shorter.

- **Camera and an extra battery:** Be ready to capture the first memories together.

- **Cell phone and charger:** Make sure you have the contact information for everyone you want to share the news with, too!

- **A lightweight pillow:** This will come in handy if you are planning to stay overnight.

WHAT YOU CAN DO...

By this time, your partner is feeling exhausted, heavy, and uncomfortable, and she probably can't wait for the pregnancy to finallybe over—and to welcome the baby, of course! Here's how you can help her thrive:

Support Your Partner

- **Let her rest:** She's getting up several times a night to pee and can't find a comfortable position. Let her sleep as much as possible and do the household chores yourself. **Be her driver:** Even if she insists she can walk somewhere, offer to drive her around so she doesn't needto waddle.

- **Connect with your baby:** Talk to them, sing to them, and touch the belly.

- **Understand her moods:** Your partner's sex drive is usually lower now since she's experiencing discomfort and can't recognize her body. Be sympathetic, and replace love- making with cuddles and massages.

- **Install the car seat:** You must have the device properly installed and checked to ensure that you can drive the baby home safely. Do it ahead of time!

- **Help her pack:** Use the hospital bag list provided earlier in this chapter.

- **Stock up the freezer:** Cook ahead for the first days at home with the newborn. Things are going to be crazy!

- **Learn the fastest route:** Study your map for when the time comes to take her to the hospital.

- **Do fun stuff together:** The time being just the two of you is almost over as you're about to become a family. Make the best of your last weeks as a single couple with no kids!

- **Pre-register at the hospital:** Help your partner with all the necessary paperwork in advance so that when the day comes, you won't have to increase your anxiety by filling out any forms.

Nursery Room and Essentials

The first time you have a baby, you may feel overwhelmed when you learn about the huge stock of baby gear you'll need to buy. Take a deep breath, call your friends and family to let them know you've registered, and get some second-hand or borrowed items if you are on a tight budget.

Some couples decide to start decorating the baby's nursery during their pregnancy, while others wait until after the baby is born, either because they are still to find out about the baby's sex or because they are planning to share their room with the baby forthe first months. Remember that if you are planning on painting and setting up a room, that's a whole lot of work and you'll hardly have the time to do it while taking care of a newborn, so my suggestion is to at least start ahead!

If possible, choose a calm, quiet space with natural light for your baby. Keep the baby close to your bedroom so you don't have to walk around the house when they get you up at night. Choose light colors for the walls, curtains, and ceiling, and avoid carpets, which can cause allergies. Most importantly: Make sure the nursery is completely safe for the baby! Have an electrician check sockets and wiring, attach furniture to the wall to prevent the baby from accidentally knocking anything down, and baby-proof thespace.

INTERACTIVE ELEMENT: BABY CHECKLIST

What do you need to buy for your baby? Some items are truly basic, while others can be included on your wish list, but you can do without them. Some are for right away (like the mandatory car seat) and others can wait (your baby won't need a chair until they are 4 or 5 months old). Here's a checklist for you to decide which items to buy, borrow, or ask for a present:

- crib or cradle

- firm, flat mattress

- 3–4 sets of fitted crib sheets

- chest of drawers or a baby wardrobe

- changing table and cleaning supplies (diapers, wipes, diaper cream, cotton, etc.)

- comfortable chair for your partner to sit and feed the baby

- baby monitor

- play mat

- toy chest or basket

- baby bathtub plus shampoo, body wash, and soft towels

KEY TAKEAWAYS

We've seen how the third trimester can be uncomfortable for your partner and a source of anxiety for both as you prepare to welcome your baby. Taking antenatal classes, packing the hospital bag, and enjoying the time spent together are great ways to make these weeks go faster. Before you know it, the big day has arrived! Let's read about delivery in the next chapter.

IT'S THE DAY

That morning, while she was having breakfast, Juliet experienced a sudden pain in the back. Daniel remembered something the doula had told them during antenatal classes. "Whatif it's a contraction?" he said. Although Juliet felt it was still earlyfor delivery since her due date was two weeks later, they bothagreed to get a check-up at the hospital just in case. Daniel put thehospital bag in the trunk of the car and breathed in relief as henoticed the baby car seat he had already installed. While he droveher through one of the three routes he had practiced, Juliet tookadvantage of those minutes to go through her birth plan once more.

I wish I had known as much as him when I became a dad for the first time! My wife's water broke in the middle of the night. Back then, cell phones weren't as common, and we didn't have the doctor's number, so we had to call him home and wake him up. He told us she shouldn't wait and he'd meet us at the hospital. That's when I remembered I'd never driven there before! And there wasn't a GPS to guide me! To make things worse, we hadn't made arrangements for the neighbor to feed our dog, so that's another person we had to get out of bed before sunrise.

As you can see, when delivery day comes, you can't have everything under control, but the more you can plan, the fewer reasons you'll have to stress about so you can focus on what's really important: taking care of your partner and get ready to meet your baby. Let's go through the basics of what you'll get through that day!

WHAT HAPPENS WHEN...

By the time the big day arrives, you'll feel more confident knowing you are prepared. This doesn't mean everything will go exactly as you plan! For example, your partner may decide she does want an epidural in the end because the pain is too much to handle. Doctors could decide it's better to opt for a C-section because the baby moved, and it's not in the best position for a vaginal delivery. Or, labor could last for hours and hours! That's why flexibility isthe key to success. It will help you stay calm and strong to better support your partner when she needs you the most.

It's Time

With the impressive list of symptoms women have during each stage of pregnancy, you may wonder whether you or your partner will be able to recognize if labor has finally started. How can you tell some other random pregnancy discomfort from the real thing? Some specific signals indicate the due date is approaching, butthere's no rush to get to the hospital yet. These include:

- **Dilation and cervix change:** During the cervical exam, doctors will check on your partner to notice any early signs of labor. Near the delivery date, the cervix becomes softer and thinner. During delivery, it will dilate up to 10 centimeters to allow the baby to go out.

- **Braxton Hicks:** Your partner may have been feeling them all the second half of the pregnancy, but they become more often and more intense in the end. The main difference with real contractions is their frequency, intensity, and location. Unlike real contractions, Braxton Hicks ones are irregular and decrease when your partner changes her position. When in doubt, ask her to sit or lie down for a while.

- **Stomach issues:** Although indigestion and heartburn are common pregnancy symptoms, pay attention if your partner has a sudden bout of diarrhea or nausea, as some women experience them 48 to 24 hours before labor begins (Health Partners, 2021). According to certified midwife Rachel Lieberman, "That's the body's way of emptying the bowels so the uterus will contract well" (Stein et al., 2022).

- **Losing the mucus plug:** Your partner may notice a single mucus-like discharge coming from her vagina or an increment in her usual discharge. However, some women lose the plug days or even weeks before giving birth, and some others don't notice it at all.

- **Loose-feeling joints:** This is due to the increment of the hormone relaxin, which is good news for the pelvis as it will stay flexible and stretch, but bad news for your partner as she feels uncomfortable, clumsy, and wobbly.

- **Baby drops:** The baby starts descending the birth canal, which creates pelvic pressure, but a positive side effect is a relief in the diaphragm and easier breathing for your partner.

- **No more weight gain:** The baby has reached their birth size, and there's less amniotic fluid than a few weeks ago.

- In her next weekly check-up, your partner may be surprised that she weighs the same as the previous week.

As the due date arrives, here are the signs and symptoms to watch for. If any of these happen, then yes, by all means, take your partner to the hospital and carry the bag with you because it's baby time:

- **Real contractions:** Early labor contractions are mild and irregular, similar to Braxton-Hicks, but they become more intense and frequent as your partner advances towards active labor. That's why it's a good idea to time contractions and the intervals between them. You can use an app or the stopwatch from your phone. How do they feel? Tell her they'll remind her of intense menstrual cramps.

- **Consistent pain in the lower back or belly:** Although backache is normal to some degree during the late stages of pregnancy, some women experience pain or cramping in their lower backs that move in waves toward the front. They are most likely labor contractions. Additionally, the way the baby is placed can influence where your partner feels more pain. There's something called "back labor" pain that happens when the baby's head puts pressure on the mother's tailbone and spine (Health Partners, 2021).

- **Bloody show:** If her increment in vaginal discharge comes in pinkish or brownish tones, it's a good indicator of the cervix changes and labor imminently approaching.

- **The water breaks:** It's the typical scenario you picture, and I blame romantic comedies! You and your partner are enjoying a candlelight dinner when suddenly... splash! She spills water like a balloon. In real life, your partner is more likely to experience this in the final moments of labor, already in the hospital. "For most women, membranes rupture, and amniotic fluid leaks after other labor symptoms have already begun. And you won't necessarily lose it all in one big gush, either—for some women, waterbreaking feels more like a trickle" (Donaldson-Evans, 2021). Water breaking is, nonetheless, an irreversible sign of labor, so you should head to the hospital anyway.

Additionally, always call the doctor (no matter how far your partner is into the pregnancy) if she experiences:

- **Bleeding or a bright red discharge:** Unlike the pink or brownish bloody show, this is a sign of a problem, and your partner should get immediate medical treatment.

- **Water comes out green or brown**: These colors indicate the presence of meconium, your baby's first stool, which can be dangerous if they ingest it. Labor must happen, and it must happen fast.

- **Blurred or double vision:** It's a common sign of preeclampsia, pregnancy-induced high blood pressure, which has to be treated right away. If the pregnancy is full-term, doctors may opt for inducing labor.

- **Severe headache:** A mild headache that goes away with Tylenol (acetaminophen) can be due to her anxiety and lack of a proper night's sleep. But a sudden, intense headache can also be a symptom of high blood pressure.

- **Sudden swelling:** Another common sign of preeclampsia to watch out for.

It's normal for couples to rush to the hospital when there's still plenty of time, especially if this is their first baby. Sometimes, they are told to go home after checking everything is okay, and it can be disappointing to come back with still no baby. But don't let this fear keep you from having your partner checked if you have any doubts! It's better to be safe than sorry.

You Arrive in the Hospital

Before going to the hospital, check with your partner's ob-gyn or midwife. They'll be able to tell if you need to rush or if there's still time. Finally, they tell you to take her there. You were able to spot the signals and remember the fastest route to the hospital or birthing center of choice. Luckily, you made it on time! No baby has come out of your partner's body yet, right? So far, so good. What should you do now?

In your hospital bag, you've packed insurance information, and you've probably filled in lots of paperwork the days before when you pre-registered, providing them with all the necessary information in advance about your partner, her medical history, her doctor, and your baby's doctor. But if your partner begins labor unexpectedly—in the case of premature birth—you'll have to fill in a lot of forms. In some cases, no matter how much you plan, the hospital staff may still ask you to do some paperwork or to fill out some more forms again. Take a deep breath and do it; don't overload your partner with your frustration!

Once you arrive at the hospital, it's a good idea to be familiarized with the different entrances. Instead of going to the emergency room (ER), you will take your partner to labor and delivery, provided that she's not experiencing some of the symptoms considered risky (such as strong bleeding or high blood pressure).

There, a nurse will take her to a triage room to evaluate how far she's into labor. Unless, of course, she comes in screaming, and she's obviously about to give birth! Additionally, if your partner is having a scheduled induction or C-section, the doctor will tell you when to arrive, and your partner will be admitted without triage.

Then, she'll have a fetal monitor hooked into her belly, a device that checks both the baby's heart rate and her contractions. Her cervix will also be checked to see if she has dilated. If her water hasn't broken yet and there are still no signs of progress, this is the point when you could be sent back home (Donovan Mauer, 2017). Never mind! You'll be back pretty soon. If there are labor contractions and some dilation, your partner will be admitted.

Once given a room, she'll have to change her clothes and wear a hospital gown. Take it easy; things could move slowly from here as contractions become more frequent and her cervix fully dilates! This is the moment when you take out your music and video games, the birth ball, the scented candles, or anything that can help her spend the hours as comfortably as possible. A nurse will periodically check on her to see how she and the baby are doing.

What happens afterward depends on whether she asked for an epidural, opioid IV medication, or no medication at all. With an epidural, she may need to wait for the anesthesiologist to arrive. After being administered, she won't be able to stand, so she will spend the rest of the waiting in bed, constantly monitored and being given fluids through an IV. If she waits before receiving it or straight skips medication, she can deal with the pain in natural ways, such as walking around, changing positions, taking a shower, and so on.

How long will you have to wait before the baby is born? Well, it's a long, long wait! Typically, labor takes about 12 to 18 hours if this is your first baby (*What to Expect in the Delivery Room*, n.d.). Don't expect the nurse to spend all her shift in the room with you and your partner. For most of the labor, the two of you will be on your own, with another person you decided to bring along, or with the doula if you hired one. Your partner's doctor isn't likely to checkon her until it's almost showtime!

Delivery Room

As hours go by, contractions will become more intense and frequent. Don't be surprised if your partner decides she wants some pain relief after all! Soon, the cervix will be fully dilated (10 centimeters), and she will feel the urge to push. At this stage of active labor, she will receive the assistance of a nurse and eitherher doctor or midwife, who will tell her exactly when to push. This may take either a couple of attempts or a couple of hours—in any case, in the final push, they will guide the baby out of the birthcanal and—there! You are finally a dad!

This is what happens if your partner has a vaginal birth and everything goes fine. However, if after long, painful contractions, your partner's cervix isn't dilating or if, when monitoring the baby, they notice any signs of fetal distress, doctors may indicate an emergency C-section. Reassure your partner that it is for the best! It doesn't matter if labor doesn't go according to plan as long as she and the baby are okay. Although a C-section is a surgery, it can still be a family-friendly experience and a celebration of bringing your child into the world.

C-Section

What happens during a C-section? The nurse will prepare your partner by removing any jewelry, shaving or clipping her pubic hair, and cleaning her skin with anti-bacterial wipes. She'll receive anesthesia—if she already had an epidural, she might be given an extra dose. General anesthesia, in which your partner is asleep, is only used in emergencies (1% of births), so most times, women are awake and fully conscious to receive their babies (*Unplanned Cesarean Delivery*, n.d.). As for you, you'll get dressed in special clothes and be by her side. Take your camera to create memories of your child's first moments!

If the C-section is scheduled for any reason, it won't be beforeweek 39 of the pregnancy. The doctor will give you instructions on how to prepare for the procedure. For example, your partner needs to eat

8 hours before the procedure and drink fluids up to 3 hours prior. You'll arrive at the hospital 2.5 hours before the scheduled time. At the delivery room, she'll receive the same preparation. The surgery takes about an hour. The baby comes out through an incision in your partner's abdomen and uterus afterthe first 15 minutes, and the rest of the time is for carefully closing the surgical incision (Fink, 2021). Don't worry; neither of you will have to see it since a curtain blocks the sight of the surgery while your partner lies awake. She may feel pressure and some pushingas the doctor guides the baby out, but it won't hurt her. And then, both your partner and the baby spend two more hours recovering, skin-to-skin, getting to know each other, and enjoying their first moments together.

Induction

We've seen what happens during natural vaginal birth and C-sections. Is there another birthing option? Yes, there is. Sometimes, doctors opt for a birth induction, which is a way to induce vaginal birth by supplying medications to your partner. First, alittle pill is inserted into her vagina near the cervix. Then, the baby gets monitored for a couple of hours to make sure they are perfectly fine. If there are no changes in the cervix after a while,you two may be sent home to wait. If the cervix dilates, the doctor may proceed to break the bag of water, and your partner will be given another medication called Pitocin through an IV to stimulate contractions (Fink, 2021). Labor will progress from then on, and if everything goes according to plan, she'll deliver the baby as in any other vaginal birth.

After Birth

The first time you see your baby, you may be amazed by their appearance. Their blue or mottled skin is covered in amniotic fluid, the cheesy vernix, and blood. Don't worry! It's all normal, and they'll become rosy pink as they take their first breaths. Your partner will feel immediate relief after the baby comes out, but she's not done yet. Some minutes after giving birth, she'll deliver the placenta, which looks like a huge piece of meat. It won't hurt her! Then, it's the time to cut the umbilical cord—and you may be offered to do so! Snip-snap and... there! Your baby is an independent person.

Shortly after birth, your baby will be dried and warmed, all within your sight, and given to you and your partner as soon as possible. If your partner had a C-section, your baby will be placed in her arms, or skin-to-skin, as you move together as a family to recovery. Most newborns naturally attempt breastfeeding during their first minutes of life. Your partner won't have milk yet, but colostrum, a rich substance that protects the baby with only some drops.

What will doctors do to your newborn? Besides weighing and measuring them, they give them a shot of vitamin K (because it is deficient in some babies) and measure their Apgar scores, which is an observation made 1 minute and 5 minutes after birth to see how well the baby is adapting to life outside the uterus. Apgar scores evaluate the baby's heart rate, breathing, color, muscle tone, and reflexes.

After you are all moved to the hospital room, your baby will spend most of their first 24 hours sleeping as they recover from birth. However, they'll also pee and poo! The first deposition is called meconium. It is dark and sticky and quite difficult to wipe! Most hospitals keep the mother and newborn together all the time, although you can ask a nurse to take the baby away for a short time to sleep or for the new mom to shower.

During the first week after birth—sometimes before getting discharged from the hospital—babies undergo a series of tests called newborn screening, which is required in all U.S. states for at least 21 disorders and in most states for additional ones (de Bellefonds, 2022). Doctors perform blood, hearing, and heart tests on your baby. These tests are meant to detect rare but potentially serious health conditions (such as metabolism or endocrinal disorders) that can be treated if detected early. These tests are perfectly safe for your baby, and most of them are at least partially covered by your health insurance, so make sure to check.

What about your partner? She needs to recover after delivery or C-section. She'll experience a variety of symptoms both if she had a vaginal birth or a C-section, and she may need to take care of her stitching, keeping either her perineum or her incision clean and disinfected. Even if she had a natural birth, she may need stitches if she had an episiotomy or experienced some tearing. During the first few days, she will go through:

- red, heavy bleeding from her vagina (called lochia)

- after-birth pains, as the uterus contracts back to its normal size

- sore nipples or breast tenderness, as she'll spend several hours a day breastfeeding

- exhaustion

- a roller coaster of emotions due to her lack of sleep, hormonal rush, and mixed feelings about becoming a first-time mom (like yourself, she's excited and grateful but also scared!)

WHAT YOU CAN DO

Giving birth is a lot for any woman! Luckily, she'll have your support to go through these first weeks of adjustment. You'll learn to be a family together.

Support Your Partner

Knowing what your partner and baby will likely go through should help ease some of your stress. After all, your primary role in the delivery room is supporting your partner, not adding up to her anxiety! Besides, you need to take care of your mental health to stay in your best version for the sake of your new family. What can you do?

- If possible, visit the delivery room during your hospital tour. "While there's very little you'll be able to change, creating a baseline comfort level can lower stress and anxiety on the day of delivery" (Dashiell, 2022).

- Pack lots of light entertainment to make the long hours of waiting go faster. Reassure your partner she's doing great and that it's normal for labor to take that long.

- During labor, take care of yourself. Your partner can't eat or drink, but you should stay strong and hydrated. Make sure you know where the vending machines are. Try to rest, but don't fall asleep: Your partner will never forgive you! "If your partner isn't sleeping, neither are you. That'sjust the way it goes. You stayed up 48 hours straight in college, right? You can do it again now" (The Bump, 2018).

- Turn off your cell phone when your partner is in active labor. Work calls or talking to your parents to share the news can wait!

- Watch your mouth! I know you are tired after long hours standing or massaging your partner's lower back, but complaining about any ache when she is in excruciating pain will not be well-received. Neither will your jokes or comments on how gross something is. To stay safe, only say words if they are supportive.

- Advocate for your partner. She may need your help standing for the birth plan you discussed together, or she may change her mind. In any case, make sure you support her and communicate her wishes to the doctor.

- If you are going to record the birth, discuss with your partner which angles she is okay with! While she may want to share the memories of the event with the rest of the family, she won't feel comfortable with her parents or yours seeing her crotch.

After your baby is born, your partner needs all her energy to recover her strength and breastfeed. She shouldn't do anything other than that. It's your time to get hands-on with your baby!

- Cuddle your baby, hold them, and settle them whenever your partner isn't feeding them so she'll have the chance to rest.

- Change their diapers and bathe them.

- Provide practical and emotional support to your partner. Do the housework, give her a glass of water when she's breastfeeding, and keep telling her what an amazing job she's doing.

- Remind your partner it's okay to need extra help. If things aren't going smoothly, you can talk to her doula or midwife or see a lactation consultant.

Make the Calls

Sometimes, labor doesn't turn out as expected. I don't want to scare you. Chances are everything will be okay, and even if there are complications, they can be promptly addressed and treated. You should know what kind of problems can occur, especially if it's a high-risk pregnancy, the due date is past more than two weeks, or your partner is older. In these scenarios, you may need to decide and ensure both your partner's and baby's safety and well-being.

- Labor may fail to progress when your partner's cervix doesn't dilate, the effacement is slow, the baby is too big, or she's giving birth to more than one baby. Sometimes, you only need to wait a bit longer and reassure your partner to help her relax. However, if complications happen during the active phase, doctors may opt for an intervention. The opposite complication is rapid labor, when contractions are so effective that labor happens faster than usual.

- Monitors may display signs of fetal distress, such as low levels of amniotic fluid, an irregular heartbeat, or problems with muscle tone. It means the baby doesn't appear to be doing well. In some cases, doctors need to get them out by C-section delivery to ensure the baby's status.

- Labor interventions may be needed if the baby is misplaced, such as shoulder dystocia, facing upward, or lying sideways. Doctors may need to use the forceps, manually change the baby's position, or perform a C- section.

- After birth, the baby may need oxygen or medication ifthey tested low on Apgar scores.

- Every woman loses blood during childbirth, but excessive bleeding can occur when uterine contractions aren't strong enough to compress the blood vessels where the placenta attached to the uterus. This is more common in certain pregnancy conditions, such as multiple births, placenta previa, uterine rupture, prolonged labor, hypertension, obesity, or blood-clogging disorders. Medical treatment—which can go through medication and massages to surgery—is required immediately because the bleeding can be life-threatening.

Going through medical checkups and having access to appropriate health care can prevent or resolve most of these complications. During pregnancy and delivery, always listen to your partner'shealth provider's advice and trust them. Things may not always go according to the birth plan, but you must reassure your partner it's all for the best.

This is what happened to my friends Daniel and Juliet. Doctors found out at the hospital the baby's head was unable to fit through Juliet's pelvis, something known as cephalopelvic disproportion (CPD). So, they went through a C-section, although it wasn't in the plan. Everything went great, and later that day, Juliet delivered a healthy baby girl.

KEY TAKEAWAYS

We've seen what to expect during different scenarios of givingbirth and discussed your role before, during, and after delivery. The following chapter will be about embracing your role as a new dad.

WELCOME TO FATHERHOOD

After spending an extra day at the hospital recovering from her C-section, Juliet and baby girl Amanda were finally discharged. Daniel drove them home, Amanda safely secured in the properly installed car seat, and they finally arrived at their place, where the three of them continued to bond with one another.

Juliet was exhausted, and her incision felt sore. Daniel was permanently attending to both her and the baby, and it didn't help him that the phone kept ringing. People were dying to see little Amanda! To let his partner rest, Daniel had to turn into a sort of goalkeeper with the visitors. Some of them came eager to help, and they were welcomed. They were the ones who volunteered to clean or bring homemade dinners. Some others wanted to be offered a cup of tea and do chit-chat, and they were politely sent away!

During your baby's first three months, your life will be turnedupside down—and more than once! This chapter will tell you what you should be aware of and what you should do to support your partner and spend time with your newborn.

WHAT HAPPENS IN...

If you thought pregnancy's week-by-week changes were breathtaking, wait until you see your baby growing and changing day by day! This is an overview of what you can expect.

The First Month

By the time you arrive home, your baby is a tiny little being who weighs less than when they were born. This drop in weight isnormal and reverts around their fifth day. Your baby's pediatrician will monitor them closely to see if they start gaining weight according to what's expected, together with their newborn reflexes, which show everything is right on track, and how their umbilical cord is healing. Doctors will also provide reassurance if you are concerned about your newborn's unusual appearance. Their body is all curled up because they are used to being squeezedinto the uterus, and their sex organs may be swollen because they are still holding some of your partner's hormones. You may notice certain features, such as a flattened nose or a cone head, which are due to being pulled through the birth canal.

Your baby's needs by this time are simple. Most of the time, they are either eating or sleeping! Their vision is still blurry, but they can see your face when you hold them closely. They already recognize your voice and their mom's scent. Besides supporting your partner with frequent and long sessions of breastfeeding, you are in charge of changing diapers (expect frequent poops at this stage!) and cuddling your newborn a lot.

Newborn babies sleep most of the time and can't tell apart days and nights yet. On average, babies spend around 16.5 hours asleep during their first month, but between 14 and 19 or even 20 hours is normal, too (Felton, 2021). Don't expect all this snoozing to happen at once, though. Babies sleep in short chunks, and they frequently wake to feed. They can breastfeed 8 to 12 times a day, while those who are bottle-fed can go a little longer without needing a bottle. Remind your partner to forget about the clock when it comes to feeding, as it's advisable to do it on demand to regulate milk production.

Other than feeding or sleeping, your newborn will spend plenty of time—yup—crying. It's the only means they have to express their needs! Your newborn cries because they are hungry, tired, overstimulated, cold, hot, or uncomfortable. At first, you won't be able to tell what they need, but spending a lot of time with your baby and always responding to their crying will make it easier as weeks go by. Don't worry! You can't spoil them by giving them extra affection.

The Second Month

As weeks pass, your newborn begins stretching the times they spend awake—although they still need plenty of sleep. Whenever they are fed, clean, and comfortable, try to stimulate their sensesby looking them in the eyes, singing to them, talking to them, and showing them high-contrast pictures in books and vibrant, colorful toys. A baby gym is also a great entertainment place. However, once your little one gets fussy, take them away from all the stimulation and make sure they get a good nap.

At this age, your baby will have some delightfully cute milestones. They start babbling, and at around 6 weeks, their first social smile appears (we call it "social" because younger babies sometimes smile, but only as a reflex of comfort). On the other hand, babies usually cry more, and their fussiness peaks around weeks 6 to 8. Don't worry! They will settle in about a month. In the meantime, keep calm and remember your bond with your baby is already strong enough for you to provide comfort and reassurance when they are at their crankiest.

Other milestones of the second month are discovering their hands and fingers (and taking them to their mouth) and sometimes attempting to roll. To encourage movement, make sure your little one spends 10 to 15 minutes a day in tummy time. They still feed pretty often and keep gaining weight fast, but you may notice their poopy diapers aren't as frequent. During their monthly check-up, their pediatrician will ensure appropriate growth and development.

The Third Month

Your baby is no longer a newborn by now! They control their movements better, turn their head whenever a sound calls their attention, and smile when they see your face. They have new facial expressions and cry in different ways whether they are hungry, sleepy, or scared. Although they won't speak for a long time, their babbling is more developed, and sometimes they can have "conversations" with you! During this month, your baby may delight you with their first giggles and laughter.

Babies gain better control of their heads and can lift themselves over their shoulders when lying on their tummy. They also control their hands to grab their favorite toys and sometimes clap them together. Make sure you give them plenty of time to move freely to develop these milestones.

At this age, babies still need to be fed on demand, but they can usually go longer stretches without the breast or bottle. Finding other ways to settle them is important, either by hugging them, singing to them, or whispering. Luckily, if you've followed a consistent bedtime routine, they are already differentiating days and nights and spend more time sleeping when it's dark (yay!). At this age, they are mature enough to start putting them on a schedule. However, this shouldn't be a rigid minute-to-minute plan buta routine that works for everyone around a few anchor momentsduring the day, such as taking the baby for a walk in their stroller or giving them a nice, relaxing bath before bedtime (Masters, 2023b).

How's Your Partner Doing?

The first 6 weeks after giving birth are the most difficult for your partner. Other than being super busy feeding the baby, she needs to give herself time to fully recover from labor, particularly if she went through a C-section. She will deal with a lot of typical but uncomfortable postpartum symptoms, such as bleeding, hemorrhoids, soreness from the stitches, constipation, backache, and sore nipples... you name it, you get it! At first, she won't recognizeher own body, and she may feel emotional all the time.

And since we are discussing emotions, most women experience baby blues during the first weeks, which are feelings of sadness that usually go away after a couple of weeks. However, if you notice your partner gets sadder, more anxious, stressed, and overwhelmed, or expresses she can't take care of the baby or herselfand those emotions last longer than a few weeks, you need to talkto her and her doctor—or your baby's doctor as well. These could be symptoms of postpartum depression (PPD), a common condition in women who had babies that needs immediate medical treatment. Sleep deprivation is one of the risk factors for PPD. Remind your partner to get as much sleep as possible, even in catnaps during the day.

WHAT YOU SHOULD KNOW

Let's see how you can stay prepared for these first months of being a dad, what you need to know about bringing home your little bundle of joy, and how often the baby needs to be checked up.

Checklist to Bring Baby Home and Tools Needed

- **Appropriate clothes:** How many outfits does your newborn need? On the one hand, they'll grow into a new size before you know it; on the other hand, they will likely need several changes daily! Keep around a dozen short- sleeved and long-sleeved onesies, nightgowns, socks or booties, one-piece sleepers, possibly a snowsuit if your baby is born in cold weather, and a few fancier outfits for when visitors show up. Just make sure you don't overdress your baby! Dress your newborn as you'd dress yourself. Inother words, if it's a warm spring day, you shouldn't put them that knitted vest and matching hat and socks.

- **Newborn check-up schedule:** Before leaving the hospital, check with your health provider about when the baby is due for their first check-up. Ask your baby's doctor, partner's lactation consultant, or a nurse before they discharge them.

- **Approved car seat:** Remember to have the car seat properly installed, if possible under professional supervision, as most car seats in the United States are not installed correctly (Ben-Joseph, 2018). It's the law to sit your baby in an age-appropriate car seat in the back of your car. Hospitals won't let you go with the baby unless you do! Babies should always ride cars facing backward because, in case of a crash, it's the safest position— although, yes, it may bring some tears as your baby growsup and doesn't get to see you or your partner!

- **Cradle or crib:** Although babies should share the room with their parents, they should sleep on an independent surface. Make sure your baby's mattress is flat and firm, and leave all those fluffy animals, bumpers, and covers outof their crib. You need several baby blankets, but make sure they never cover their face.

- **Feeding supplies:** Get several bottles, nipples, and formula (always check the expiration date). If your partner breastfeeds, just some nursing bras and a nursing pillow will do, although a breast pump and bags to stock milk in the freezer are also advisable.

- **Diaper supplies:** Diapers come in different sizes according to how much your baby weighs. During the first months, they could grow one or two sizes! While it's advisable to buy a diaper supply ahead of time, keep them in more than one size. You also need to stock on baby wipes and ointment.

- **Bathing supplies:** There's no need to rush into giving your baby their first bath, nor do they need to take one every day unless they enjoy it. Get a plastic infant tub that lets you carefully place the baby in a comfortable position— never leave them unsupervised in the bathtub, not for a second! You should also grab some hooded towels and baby shampoo, lotion, and soap to get your little one clean and protect their delicate skin.

- **Medical care:** Before buying any medical supplies, it's best to check with your baby's doctor. However, you will probably need a bulb syringe to help your baby get rid of mucus, nail clippers so they don't accidentally scratch themselves, anti-gas drops and acetaminophen in case they have a fever, and a thermometer.

How Much to Feed

During the first months of your baby's life, they must be fed on demand, meaning that instead of following a strict schedule, they should be given breastmilk or formula whenever they are hungry. So, let's try another question: How can you tell if your newborn is hungry? You need to learn to read their cues. Sure, if your baby is crying, they are possibly demanding to be fed, but by this point, they are starving and, therefore, are hard to settle. Earlier hunger cues include the baby licking their lips, sticking their tongue out, putting their hand to mouth, opening their mouth, puckering their lips, or rooting (moving their head or jaw searching for the breast).

How often should you feed a newborn? As a rule of thumb, the younger the infant, the more frequently they eat. This is because their tiny stomachs can't hold as much milk at once, and they need frequent refills. During their first month, babies eat between 8 and 12 times a day, and as they grow, so does their intake. "Babies might only take half an ounce per feeding for the first day or two of life, but after that, will usually drink 1 to 2 ounces at each feeding. This amount increases to 2 to 3 ounces by 2 weeks of age"(Jain, 2023). By the time your baby turns 2 months old, they usually take about 4 to 5 ounces every 3 to 4 hours. With breastfeeding, it may be hard to tell exactly how much milk your baby drinks with each intake. However, if they wet 4 to 5 diapers a day and regularly do depositions, that's an indication—together with their weight gain—that they are getting enough food.

According to their weight gain, you can tell if a baby is well fed, overfed, or underfed. Bottle-fed babies have higher chances of being overfed because it's easier for them to drink milk from a bottle. Remember that for babies, suction isn't only about getting food but also about being soothed, and this is where pacifiers are a great help!

At certain points, your baby may seem hungrier than usual. This happens when they go through a growth spurt (a period of rapid growth) and demand more food. These growth spurts usually happen at around 7 to 14 days, between 3 to 6 weeks, at 4 months, and at 6 months (Gavin, 2021). What's important is to keep feeding your baby on demand, even when it means offering them the breast or the bottle more frequently or for longer.

Postpartum Tests and Check-Ups

After bringing your baby home, you'll first get out of the house when you take them to their first check-up, which is due 3 to 5 days after birth. What can you expect from this visit? The health provider will weigh and measure your baby and check their head circumference. This is for monitoring their growth. Then, they'll ask you questions and advise you about feeding, sleeping, peeing and pooping, and overall general behavior. Then, your baby will have a general exam done—the doctor will check their eyes, hips, testicles and circumcision if it's a boy, breathing, and heart rate, review screening tests from the hospital, and update immunizations.

After that first well-baby check-up, you need to bring them again when they are about 2 weeks old, and afterward, when they are 1 month, 2 months, 4 months, and 6 months old unless indicated otherwise. You'll receive a personal child health record (PCHR), which you have to take with you whenever your baby visits their doctor or gets vaccines. You can also fill in information about their milestones and any illnesses, medicines, or accidents.

It's easy to get lost in the mist after having a baby and following up on all of their newborn check-ups, but keep in mind your partner needs medical care, too. Her body went through major trauma by carrying a pregnancy and giving birth, so she must visit her doctor as well. Sadly, 2 out of 5 new moms in the United States miss their postpartum check-ups, which leaves them vulnerable to serious, even life-threatening conditions (March of Dimes, 2023b). So, youshould insist your partner gets herself checked no matter how fine she's feeling.

The American College of Obstetricians and Gynecologists (ACOG, 2018) recommends new moms contact their health provider 3 weeks after giving birth, getting ongoing medical care as needed during recovery, and then having a complete medical check-up at week 12 after delivery. Doctors may look for symptoms of postnatal health problems, especially PPD, and give you and your partner advice for contraceptive methods.

WHAT YOU CAN DO

Now that you have an idea of what life after a baby may be like, let's see how to make the most of it.

Support Your Partner

- **Give her water:** Your partner will need lots of fluids and nutritious meals to recover and breastfeed. Whenever she's nursing the baby, give her a glass of water without asking. Make sure she stays hydrated and well-fed. If possible, prepare something she can eat with a single hand!

- **Be the ice provider:** Help her relieve the soreness of her perineal or abdominal incision by handing her fresh ice pads. While she's resting, ask her if she needs anything, from her phone to the remote control. It will make adifference!

- **Ask for family and friends to help:** Some people are willing to give both of you a hand. Some others just want cute baby pictures to post in their Instagram stories. Filter those visitors and make sure no one overextends their welcome.

- **Let her sleep in the morning:** If she's handling night feedings, try having the baby while you make breakfast and allow her those extra minutes of sleep. It will also give you the chance to spend one-on-one time with your newborn.

- **Treat her:** Now that the baby is born, they receive all the attention, and no one seems to remember the postpartum mom! Surprise her with her favorite flowers, a bar of chocolate, or a sushi take-out she couldn't enjoy for the past nine months.

- **Refrain from making comments about her body:** This means praise, too. She's not feeling herself, and if you compliment her appearance, she may believe you are being condescending or pushing her to get back to your sex life, which is the last thing on her mind right now. It's better to compliment other traits, such as her strength or how great she's doing as a new mom.

- **Watch out for PPD signals:** Talk to her. Most women keep these feelings to themselves because they feel guilty or inadequate, but it's crucial that they receive medical help. "Depression isn't something you should just 'suffer through,' and you definitely shouldn't be ashamed to get the help that you—and your baby—need" (Felton, 2021).

- **Look after your own mental health:** New dads can also suffer from anxiety or depression. In the following chapter, we'll provide tips for self-care for new dads.

Spend Time With Baby

Your partner is the one with the boobs, but soon you'll discover new dads have other baby superpowers! The longer you spend with your newborn, the more ways you'll find to connect withthem and establish a strong, loving bond.

- **Hold your baby:** This may seem obvious, but some new dads feel inadequate or fear being too clumsy with their fragile newborn. Practice makes perfect! Be gentle, soft, and warm. Soon, your newborn will recognize you and calm down whenever you hold or cuddle them.

- **Communicate with them:** Just because they can't speak doesn't mean you can't talk to them! Tell them about your day and what you're doing. Describe objects around the house. Smile at them and look them into their eyes. It's never too early to start reading or singing to a baby.

- **Respond to their crying:** Hold your baby gently when they cry, even if you don't know why they are crying. By doing so, you are letting them know they can count on you.

- **Watch for their cues:** When you spend a lot of time with your baby, it becomes easier to understand their needs and respond accordingly. Take a mental note of how they behave when hungry or sleepy. Soon, you'll be able to decipher their cues.

- **Keep them safe:** Learning to wrap your baby is a way of keeping them comfortable and secure.

- **Develop daddy codes:** Singing your own tunes, making silly faces, and being goofy around your baby will soon become part of your unique role as a dad. Your newborn may not respond immediately, but just wait for their first smile and giggles; they will melt your heart.

INTERACTIVE ELEMENT: HOW-TO STEPS

You'll learn to take care of your baby with practice. If it makes you feel more secure, here are a few easy-to-remember, step-by-step instructions on some usual tasks:

Carry and Hold

1. Place one hand under your baby's head for support.

2. Slide the second hand under your baby's bottom.

3. Bend your knees to protect your back.

4. Scoop up the baby, bringing them close to your chest.

Prepare Formula

1. Check the expiration date.

2. Wash your hands.

3. Sterilize bottle and nipples.

4. Add water to the formula if it's concentrated liquid or powder. Do not overdilute.

5. Warm the formula. Test its temperature by putting a few drops on your wrist.

6. Feed the baby. The formula should be used within the hour.

7. Discard what's left in the bottle.

Swaddle

1. Spread the blanket on a firm surface, with one corner pointing up.

2. Fold the top corner down.

3. Place the baby on the swaddle.

4. Take the left side of the blanket and wrap it over your baby's arm and chest.

5. Tuck that side of the blanket underneath their back.

6. Cover your baby's body with the bottom of the blanket.

7. Tuck the right side of the blanket under their left side.

8. Check that the baby is snug, not too loose or too tight.

Burp

1. Hold your baby upright with their head resting on your shoulder.

2. Cup your free hand slightly.

3. Gently pat their back with your cupped hand.

Calm a Crying Baby

1. Always go to your baby whenever they cry.

2. Check their temperature.

3. See if they are hungry or need a new diaper.

4. Hold them close against your body and whisper calm words.

5. Rock them or walk around with them.

6. Sing to them.

7. Offer them a pacifier.

8. If everything fails, sometimes a ride in the stroller or car does wonders.

Put to Sleep

1. Learn to read your baby's tiredness cues.

2. Check that the baby is comfortable.

3. Darken the room and play white noise.

4. Swaddle your baby.

5. Place them in the crib, always on their back, when they are drowsy but still awake.

6. Offer them a pacifier.

KEY TAKEAWAYS

Now you know all the basics about bringing your baby home and what to expect during these first months as a family. Remember: Your baby needs you, but the best you can do for them is look after your partner and give her time to recover. And, speaking about your partner, our last chapter will deal with the two of you, whether you remain a couple or opt to co-parent, as well as some self-care strategies new dads should implement.

IT TAKES TIME

In previous chapters, I told you how my friends Daniel and Juliet started their family. Some decades ago, their family type—two heterosexual, married parents—was considered the norm, but nowadays, this traditional family is just one possibility. In the United States, almost 13 million custodial parents are living with children under age 21, and more than 20% of them are dads, over 2.5 million. "It's slowly becoming more likely for custodial parents to be fathers, especially compared to a few decades ago" (Lazic, 2023).

Single dads aren't something new. Even before divorce was legal, there were always some widowers, right? The novelty is that not only are divorced men actively taking the role of looking aftertheir children, but also, more men are becoming single dads *by choice*. The phenomenon is known as platonic parenting orconscious or elective co-parenting. Sarah Treleaven from *Today's Parent* describes it as "a twist on friends with benefits—the benefits, in this case, being a partner to share in the emotional, physical, psychological, and practical gauntlet of raising a child" (2021).

The favorite way for gay men to become fathers, and currently chosen by 16 million non-married people in the United States (Hope, 2024), co-parenting begins with the active search for a partner, but not in a romantic/sexual way. You look for someone to share the adventure of parenting a child, whether living under the same roof or sharing their custody. Sometimes, their kids are born through fertility treatments; other times, they are adopted. In any case, platonic parenting is becoming a new norm.

In this final chapter, we'll discuss how to integrate being a dad with your relationship with your partner—whether romantic or not—and discover the importance of self-care and how a self-care routine can help you be a better father and partner.

CAN CO-PARENTING WORK?

As mentioned before, conscious co-parenting is the arrangement two or more people make to raise a child without being romantically involved. It requires previous talks about topics related to child-rearing, such as education, religion, parenting styles, views on vaccination, and such. Co-parenting also refers to a friendly divorce in which the couple no longer remains together but keeps interacting and sharing the raising of their child.

People who co-parent need to agree on finances and living arrangements. While in some ways it happens when sharing child custody after a non-conflictive divorce, co-parenting also happens with people who aren't and have never been romantically involved with each other. Therefore, it allows them to focus entirely on the child's needs and well-being. As with any other family model, it has its ups and downs.

The Pros of Co-Parenting

Unlike parallel parenting—when two people split up and divide the custody of their children with little or no interaction with each other—when two people co-parent, they communicate frequently and work together in deciding what's best for their child(ren). Therefore, they provide a unified set of rules and discipline that secures the child by providing them with a stable environment. This is how Keoni Souza, who provides legal counseling to families, puts it: "Whether or not the parents have a romantic relationship with one another is immaterial to their ability to raise healthy and happy kids, so long as their co-parenting relationship is solid" (2019).

If co-parenting happens after a divorce, it helps diffuse tension since the adults put their conflicts aside to focus on making things work for their children. People who opt for platonic co-parenting say it has the best of both worlds. Jessica, a woman from Seattle who co-parents with her best friend from elementary school, says she and

Naomi focus on parenting and their friendship, leaving aside the usual conflicts of romantic relationships. "I think it's a lot to match with someone on parental philosophy, willingness to actually share the tasks of parenting, and then add in sexual and romantic chemistry" (Hope, 2024).

Particularly for cis-gender women, the possibility of finding a platonic co-parent relieves the pressure of the "ticking clock," as they no longer feel rushed to find a romantic partner before their age makes it challenging to become pregnant and to carry on a safe pregnancy. Some women decide to take the step by themselves, becoming single moms by choice with the help of a sperm donor. However, sharing the workload of caring for a child usually works best for them.

Platonic parents also share the financial burden of child-rearing, starting from the expensive fertility treatments and moving on with housing arrangements and child education. Sometimes, they manage to live together under the same roof (without sharing the bed); other times, their child spends equal time in both homes.

Some Cons of Co-Parenting

While co-parenting works great for some people, others state it is not for everyone. When it happens after a divorce, you need to set aside your feelings. Every possible resentment or personal conflict with your former spouse must be left behind to co-parent together. This isn't possible when the relationship is particularly conflictive. "If you continue to feel disrespected or unsafe around your ex, this can negatively affect your children as well. The emotional well-being and safety of you and your child must come first" (Dodson, 2024).

As for platonic co-parenting, it may work great, but it takes a lot of planning. And even then, expectations can change after the baby is born. What if one of the co-parents falls in love and wants to start another family? What if one of you gets a job abroad? Besides, sometimes legislation doesn't contemplate these arrangements. For example, if two LGBTQ+ couples decide to co-parent a child, depending on which state the baby is born in, the birth certificate may include only the biological parents.

How to Be a Great Co-Parenting Partner

If you are about to become a dad or have just welcomed your newborn into the world and find yourself co-parenting, you may wonder how to make things work with the other parent(s). Here are some tips for successfully co-parenting a baby:

- **If you are divorced or separated, set your feelings aside:** Consider you are starting a new relationship from scratch with your partner, one focused entirely on the benefit of your child. It's no longer about the two of you; it's about providing stability and happiness to this little person for whom you two are responsible. So, deal with your anger, resentment, or sadness, and don't let them control your actions. Talk about how you feel with a friend, family, or a professional if you need one.

- **Keep the conversations on parenting:** Avoid addressing issues like new relationships or how your ex spends their money. Refrain from making personal remarks. You need to communicate fluently, but only to talk about baby stuff. You don't always need to speak in person, as some matters can be discussed on the phone or by email. However, you must remain open and honest with each other on issues such as medical needs or education.

- **Come up with a plan:** Don't leave anything to chance. Each parent has rights and responsibilities, such as visitation schedules and baby-related expenses. Put them in a contract and stick to them. This will give you clear guidelines and strengthen the co-parenting relationship.

- **Be consistent:** Babies rely on routines. When you decide on your co-parenting schedule, consider that your baby needs frequent visits and quality time with both parents to bond. "Ensure to visit the baby several times a week. When visiting, you must use the time to bond with the infant to familiarize them with your presence. You can feed, soothe, or bathe the newborn if you want" (*Co-Parenting a Newborn*, n.d.). At the same time, consider that your arrangements don't interfere with your baby's feeding and resting times.

- **Consider taking your vacation together:** According to experts, babies and toddlers shouldn't spend too many days apart from either of their parents during their first two years (*Co-Parenting a Newborn*, 2020). While having the baby over for a long weekend is okay, if you want to take them to meet your parents in another state, it would be best to ask your partner if they agree to join you.

- **Revisit rules and expectations:** The agreement you have today may not work in the future. Those visitation schedules that work so great now may need to be redesigned as your baby enters new milestones, such as sleeping fewer naps or beginning kindergarten. Other possible changes are financial challenges (for example, if either of you suddenly lost your job) or meeting a new romantic partner.

- **Be flexible:** People grow and change, and so do families: "Just like in any other family dynamic, your co-parenting relationship and family needs will evolve during your journey, so flexibility and keeping an open mind are key" (Zielger, 2022). Allow yourself and your co-parent that room to grow.

IS SELF- CARE IMPORTANT?

Being a dad will change your life in unimagined ways. It will certainly transform your relationship with your partner, and the relationship with your child will become one of the most meaningful in your existence. However, when I became a dad, I never imagined how deeply it would impact another relationship: Thatis, the one I have with myself. Looking at my newborn, I understood she needed me at my best and would need me for manyyears to come. After becoming a father, I stopped smoking andtook exercise as a regular habit. I started eating healthier, and I went through a lot of work to heal past trauma so I could be the strong, supportive father she deserved without losing my energy fighting my demons.

Don't Suffer in Silence

Looking after your health is important, and that includes your mental health. Did you know that more than 6 million men in the United States suffer from depression? They become tired, irritable, lose interest in work, and feel worthless. This condition affectsdads specifically: 1 in 10 fathers experience PPD or anxiety, and sadly, they are less likely to receive a mental health diagnosis—and, therefore, the treatment they need—than their female partners (Fleming, 2023). New responsibilities, together with the cultural imperative to keep your problems to yourself, put men under a lot of pressure.

This mandate to "man up" only perpetuates the bias of weakness whenever a man expresses discomfort or pain. "The problem is that if men can't speak about their pain, they won't have a way to begin to process and deal with it or reach out for help. With dads, it not only impacts his own life but also his children's lives," explains

LaKeisha Fleming from Verywell Mind. It's clear: You area role model to your children. They do as they see. If you struggle with a mental health issue and they see you actively addressing it, reaching out for help, and openly talking about it with your partner or other loved ones, they'll learn to cope. However, if you hide your pain and mask it with anger, violence, or substance abuse, that's what you'll be teaching them to do in the future.

Self-Care for Dads

A lot has been said about the importance of self-care for new moms, and it's always important to underline it. In previous chapters, we've mentioned several ways in which you should support your partner during pregnancy and after giving birth. However, the only way new dads can fulfill their many new roles is by first caring for themselves. You know the old saying: You can't pour from an empty cup. You need a healthy body, mind, and happiness in your life!

The good news is that, with a little imagination, it is possible to combine self-care activities with being a father. Your child is ahuge motivator for embracing new, healthy habits and creating a new routine. Here are some ideas; you'll come up with yours as well!

- **Get a check-up:** You're probably used to driving your partner and your newborn baby back and forth to the doctor's office. Why not do it for you this time?

- **Sign up for a baby and me yoga class:** Although most are labeled "mommy and me," many yoga instructors will happily accept dads in their classes! It's a fantastic way to breathe out your worries, connect with your baby, and gain flexibility at the same time.

- **Personal grooming:** Make shaving a ritual. Invest in a good lotion and moisturizer. Taking care of the skin isn'tjust for the ladies, you know.

- **Eat healthy:** Since you are doing most of the cooking, seize the opportunity to include more fruits, vegetables, whole grains, and a variety of healthy foods in your diet. Ordering a pizza once a week won't kill you, but a homemade casserole tastes way better!

- **Build a dad community:** Having solid friendships is important for your mental health. While it's natural for some friends to distance themselves after you become a dad, having a child also creates new opportunities for youto make new friends. Go talk to other dads by the swings or organize a barbecue with the families from daycare.

- **Make time for your hobbies:** You won't spend much time building a scale model once your baby is a newborn. Still, as their sleep schedule becomes slightly less erratic, save some time for doing the things you like.

- **Get enough sleep:** This is easier said than done. But one thing is getting out of bed to change your baby so your partner can get some shut-eye, and another is spending those precious hours you could be in bed scrolling down your phone. Practice good sleep hygiene habits and get asmuch rest as possible.

- **Spend time outdoors:** Being surrounded by nature does wonders for your mental health! Taking your baby in the stroller for a walk is a perfect way to get some exercise, fresh air, and quality time together.

- **Cut down on social media and turn on the music:** Did you know that screen time is bad for your baby? Then, why would it be good for yourself? On the other hand, music significantly improves your well-being and lowersyour heart rate and blood pressure (Dolan, 2023).

- **Find professional help:** Finally, if you feel it's too much to take on, never hesitate to reach out to a therapist. It doesn't make you any less of a man, and it will turn you into a better dad.

MAKING TIME FOR YOUR REL ATIONSHIPS

When baby Amanda was 6 months old, Daniel and Juliet finally went on a date. As they toasted with a mocktail, they looked at each other. They barely recognized the person in front of them! Having a baby changes the relationship's dynamics in so many ways! Some are obvious (you knew your partner wouldn't be in the mood for love-making after delivering a 6-pound baby!), and others come totally unexpected.

Couples who have a baby often find themselves constantly arguing. Sleep deprivation, stress, and constant demands from the newborn mean you have less patience than ever and that you don't put your relationship first anymore. Communication becomes merely practical—instead of texting each other "I love U" or fun memes, you replace them with "Get more formula" or "Ped today 2 p.m." Having a baby doesn't leave room for spontaneity—nor energy for your sex life! Both of you crave for "me" time. And ifyou add your colliding parenting styles, the unavoidable money issues, and grandparents dropping by unexpectedly, well, thereyou have it! No wonder why the biggest challenge for new parents is not getting divorced, right?

Look at the bright side, though: You've been through a lot, which means you're now stronger than before! Plus, you can do some things to help you work on the relationship and make time for yourselves even after a baby. Here are some tips:

- **Talk about how you feel:** Share how you're living every experience without necessarily expecting the other person to fix things or to have everything figured out. Simply open up about both the joy and rewards, as well as the pain, the struggles, and the doubts.

- **Share some special time**: Maybe you can't plan date nights or go to concerts. But you can share a cup of coffee after a long night taking shifts with your newborn, watch a short sitcom episode, and laugh together when the baby is finally asleep.

- **Work as a team:** This means equally dividing tasks, being kind to one another, and praising each other for your efforts.

- **Set clear boundaries with your extended families**: If now that you have a baby, your parents or in-laws are constantly dropping by, it's time to have a talk and decide how to manage visits. It may work out for the best! Maybe they are so excited about seeing the new baby that they can babysit instead of waiting to be offered some coffee.

- **Be specific:** Instead of complaining about your partner's attitude, ask for specific changes in their behavior. For example, replace "I'm tired of keeping track of everything!" with "Please, include the baby checkups in your calendar app."

- **Get physical:** Maybe sex is still off the table. But you can reconnect by kissing, cuddling, or giving your partner a back rub. Physical intimacy is the key to a healthy, loving relationship.

- **Expand the meaning of "dates":** Maybe you aren't ready to go out to a restaurant and leave the baby with anyone else. But you can still make some time for each other. For example, you can order take-out and set a nice table at home when the baby is out for the night, or you can drop by and surprise your partner on her lunch break at work with a lovely bouquet.

- **Play games:** Plan a game night with your partner instead of automatically turning on the TV. Board games or video games, what matters is having fun together!

- **Create new family routines:** Taking the baby for a walk in the evening, getting in the car and visiting a farmer's market every other Saturday, or eating lunch in the backyard can become new rituals to bring you closer bothas a couple and as a family of three.

Be patient with yourself and kind to your partner. It will take time to adjust and find a "new normal." Even then, you'll still face problems and challenges, but tackling them before they get worse is essential. Remember that you can get professional help if you feel stuck and things start falling apart. But working on your relationship isn't just important for the two of you. Communicating and making time can help you be better parents to your newborn baby.

KEY TAKEAWAYS

We've seen how to be there for your baby even if you aren't involved in a romantic relationship with your co-parenting partner. Remember that self-care and making time for your relationship are equally important for happily fulfilling your new role asa dad.

SHARE YOUR WISDOM, SHAPE A DAD' S JOURNEY

Embrace the Magic of Giving Back

"A little kindness goes a long way."

— UNKNOWN

People who lend a hand without expecting anything in return often find greater joy and fulfillment in life. So, let's give it a whirl!

Now, let me ask you this...

Would you lend your support to someone you've never met, even if you didn't receive recognition for it?

Who might this person be? Well, they're a lot like you. Or, at least, like the younger you—curious, a bit nervous, and hungry for knowledge but not quite sure where to find it.

My mission? To make the journey of impending fatherhood a breeze for dads like you. Every word I write stems from this mission. And, the only way for me to fulfill it is by reaching...well... everyone.

And this is where you come into play. It's true what they say— people often judge a book by its cover (and its reviews). So here's my humble plea on behalf of a struggling first-time dad you've yet to meet:

Would you consider leaving a review for this book? Simply scan the QR code below to leave your review:

Your act of kindness won't cost a penny and requires just a minute of your time, yet it holds the power to transform a fellow dad's life. Your review might just...

Provide invaluable guidance during pregnancy, fostering confidence and strengthening familial bonds.

To Leave A Review Go To:

Amazon.com

- Or Scan Below -

CONCLUSION

You've reached the end of the book, but your parenting journey has just begun, and it is meant to last a lifetime. Being a father, especially being as involved as millennial dads are, is always a challenge. Hopefully, you are better prepared to face this lifelong adventure by now! By applying the lessons you learned from this book, be confident you will be a fantastic dad. Anytime you feel in doubt, remember the CRAFT method: Consider, Recognize, Awareness, Fatherhood, and Time. Think of it as a guideline as you enter fatherhood.

I hope you'll find some of the tips and suggestions provided helpful. There's no single answer to how to be a dad, as it's different for each one. You'll come up with your own unique way. However, having a guide to help you through pregnancy and beyond will help ease your doubts and gain confidence in your parenting skills. I promise: It gets easier in time.

Thank you for letting me walk you through this journey. One final request: If you enjoyed the book, kindly leave a review to help me reach out to new dads-to-be.

Happy parenting!

GLOSSARY

Amniotic sac: The bag of water that protects the baby inside the uterus.

Apgar: A quick test performed on the baby during the first minutes after birth.

Baby blues: Mood swings experienced by most women in the first weeks after giving birth.

Blastocyst: The cluster of cells that will eventually develop into an embryo.

Braxton-Hicks: These are "training" contractions that a pregnant woman can feel throughout the second half of the pregnancy. Unlike real contractions, they are irregular and fade when the woman changes her position or rests.

Colostrum: The first form of milk produced by the woman's breasts immediately after giving birth. It is the newborn's first food.

Fertility cliff: A theoretical point in a lifetime when the ability to get pregnant decreases.

Fertility window: The five days before ovulation and the day of ovulation are the moments when a couple can conceive a baby.

HCG: Human chorionic gonadotropin is a pregnancy-induced hormone that can be tracked in blood or a home urine pregnancy test.

Lanugo: A soft layer of hair the fetus grows during the second trimester, which covers their entire skin and keeps them protected.

Lochia: Heavy vaginal bleeding that happens after giving birth.

Meconium: The baby's first deposition after birth.

Ovulation: The process in which a woman's ovary releases an egg. It usually happens once a month, around 2 weeks before a woman's period.

PPD: Postpartum depression. It's a frequent condition a woman can experience after giving birth when baby blues doesn't naturally get better. It requires medical treatment.

Preeclampsia: A common pregnancy-induced disease usually noticeable by high blood pressure.

Zygote: The unique, single-cell product of fecundation of a sperm and an egg.

BIBLIOGRAPHY

After your baby is born: for partners of birthing mothers. (n.d.). Raising Children Network. https://raisingchildren.net.au/pregnancy/pregnancy-for-partners/early-parenting/after-your-baby-is-born-for-partners

The American College of Obstetricians and Gynecologists. (2018, May). Optimizing postpartum care. https://www.acog.org/clinical/clinical-guidance/committeeopinion/articles/2018/05/optimizing-postpartum-care

Antenatal classes - preparing you for the birth. (n.d.). Tommy's. https://www.tommys.org/pregnancy-information/im-pregnant/antenatal-care/antenatal-classespreparing-you-birth

Antenatal classes. (2023, May). Pregnancy, Birth, & Baby. https://www.pregnancybirthbaby.org.au/antenatal-classes

Antenatal classes. (2024, January 17). NHS. https://www.nhs.uk/pregnancy/labourand-birth/preparing-for-the-birth/antenatal-classes/

Are you pregnant? Here are the early signs and symptoms of pregnancy. (2021). Health Partners. https://www.healthpartners.com/blog/first-symptoms-of-pregnancy/

Ayuda, T. (2021, August 17). What to expect from third-trimester prenatal appointments. Babycenter. https://www.babycenter.com/pregnancy/health-and-safety/thirdtrimester-prenatal-visits_9346

Batcha, B. & Srinivasan, H. (2023, January 5). A nine-month plan for getting your fami-ly's finances in order pre-baby. Parents. https://www.parents.com/pregnancy/considering-baby/financing-family/a-nine-month-plan-for-getting-yourfamilys-finances-in-order-pre-baby/

Baby's first 24 hours. (2022, September). Pregnancy, Birth & Baby. https://www.pregnancybirthbaby.org.au/babys-first-24-hours

Bean, S. (2019). Parenting responsibilities: 10 things you are (and aren't) responsible for as a parent. Empowering Parents. https://www.empoweringparents.com/article/parenting-responsibilities-10-things-you-are-and-arent-responsible-for-as-aparent/

Ben-Joseph, E.P. (2018, June). Bringing your baby home. Kids Health. https://kidshealth.org/en/parents/bringing-baby-home.html

Ben-Joseph, E.P. (2022, July). Your child's checkup: 3 to 5 days. Kids Health. https://kidshealth.org/en/parents/checkup-2weeks.html

Bogle, J. (2021, August 10). 11 ways dads can practice self-care and why they should (yes, even you!). The Dad. https://www.thedad.com/dads-self-care/

Bonding and attachment: newborns. (2018). Raising Children Network. https://raisingchildren.net.au/newborns/connecting-communicating/bonding/bondingnewborns

Brewster, A. (2023, July 5). How to support your partner after birth. Today's Parent.https://www.todaysparent.com/baby/postpartum-care/how-to-support-yourwife-after-birth/

The Bump. (2018, February 28). He said WHAT in the delivery room? Tips for dads on delivery day. https://www.thebump.com/a/he-said-what-in-the-delivery-room

Can I get pregnant just after my period has finished? (2021, July 8). NHS. https://www.nhs.uk/common-health-questions/pregnancy/can-i-get-pregnant-just-aftermy-period-has-finished/

Case, H. (n.d.). *7 things you need when bringing Baby home.* Kinsa Health. https://home.kinsahealth.com/post/7-things-you-need-when-bringing-baby-home

Choosing the right healthcare provider for pregnancy and childbirth. (2022). MedLinePlus. https://medlineplus.gov/ency/patientinstructions/000596.htm

Cleveland Clinic. (2022a, November 28). *Pregnancy tests.* https://my.clevelandclinic.org/health/diagnostics/9703-pregnancy-tests

Cleveland Clinic. (2022b, November 14). *Pregnancy complications.* https://my.clevelandclinic.org/health/articles/24442-pregnancy-complications

Cleveland Clinic. (2023). *Fetal development.* https://my.clevelandclinic.org/health/articles/7247-fetal-development-stages-of-growth

Common tests during pregnancy. (n.d.). John Hopkins Medicine. https://www.hopkinsmedicine.org/health/wellness-and-prevention/common-tests-during-pregnancy

Co-parenting a newborn. (n.d.). 2 Houses. https://www.2houses.com/en/blog/coparenting-a-newborn-how-to-do-it-successfully

Co-parenting a newborn. (2020, October 8). Talking Parents. https://talkingparents.com/parenting-resources/coparenting-a-newborn

Cross, C.I. (2022). *Why can't I get pregnant?* John Hopkins Medicine. https://www.hopkinsmedicine.org/health/conditions-and-diseases/why-cant-i-get-pregnant

Dad-to-be guide: 10 facts for the third trimester. (2019). NCT. https://www.nct.org.uk/pregnancy/dads-be/dad-be-guide-10-facts-for-third-trimester

Dashiell, C. (2022, April 8). 4 essential tips for men who are new to the delivery room. Fatherly. https://www.fatherly.com/parenting/dads-delivery-room-stress

de Bellefonds, C. (2022, February 14). Newborn screenings: What tests will my baby get in the hospital? What to Expect. https://www.whattoexpect.com/first-year/health-and-safety/newborn-screening-tests-and-procedures/

Deibel, P.T. (2020, March 23). Pregnant? Here are 4 things to think about when choosing a doctor or midwife. UNC Health Talk. https://healthtalk.unchealthcare.org/pregnant-here-are-4-things-to-think-about-when-choosing-a-doctor-or-midwife/

Dodson, J. (2024, February 20). What is co-parenting? The pros and cons to consider. Better Help. https://www.betterhelp.com/advice/parenting/what-is-co-parenting-the-pros-and-cons-to-consider/

Dolan, M. (2023, June 5). The 8 best things dads can do for themselves in honor of Father's Day. Everyday Health. https://www.everydayhealth.com/healthy-living/best-things-dads-can-do-for-themselves-in-honor-of-fathers-day/

Donaldson-Evans, C. (2023a, October 5). 1 & 2 weeks pregnant. What to Expect. https://www.whattoexpect.com/pregnancy/week-by-week/weeks-1-and2.aspx

Donaldson-Evans, C. (2023b, October 5). 17 weeks pregnant. What to Expect. https://www.whattoexpect.com/pregnancy/week-by-week/week-17.aspx

Donaldson-Evans, C. (2023c, October 5). 40 weeks pregnant. What to Expect.?

Donaldson-Evans, C. (2021, August 6). Signs of labor. What to Expect. https://www.whattoexpect.com/pregnancy/labor-signs

Donovan Mauer, E. (2017, May 17). What happens at the hospital when you deliver? The Bump.

https://www.thebump.com/a/what-to-expect-at-the-hospitalduring-labor

Felton, K. (2021, October 25). Baby month 1: Your newborn guide. What to Expect. https://www.whattoexpect.com/first-year/month-1

Fink, J. (2021, August 14). Labor and delivery: What to expect at the hospital. Health-grades. https://www.healthgrades.com/right-care/pregnancy/labor-and-delivery-what-to-expect-at-the-hospital

First trimester: Tips for dads to be. (2019). NCT. https://www.nct.org.uk/pregnancy/dads-be/first-trimester-tips-for-dads-be

Five factors to consider whether you are ready for a baby. (n.d.) IFEC. https://www.ifec.org.hk/web/en/other-resources/hot-topics/5-factors-to-consider-whetheryou-are-ready-for-a-baby.page

Fleming, L. (2023, June 13). We can't ignore our dads' mental health, even if they try to. Verywell Mind. https://www.verywellmind.com/dads-mental-health-matters5409299

Foods to avoid when pregnant. (2019). Pregnancy Birth & Baby. https://www.pregnancybirthbaby.org.au/foods-to-avoid-when-pregnant

From newborn to 15 months old, here's your new baby's checkup schedule. (2021). HealthPartners. https://www.healthpartners.com/blog/well-baby-visits-schedule/

Fuentes, A. (2018, August). Prenatal test: First trimester screening. Kids Health. https://kidshealth.org/en/parents/prenatal-screen.html

Gavin, M.L. (2021, November). Formula feeding FAQs: How much and how often. KidsHealth. https://kidshealth.org/en/parents/formulafeed-often.html

Geddes, J. K. (2021, June 14). *How to create a birth plan. What to Expect.* https://www.whattoexpect.com/pregnancy/labor-and-delivery/birth-plan/

Geddes, J.K. (2023, October 25). *Hospital bag checklist. What to Expect.* https://www.whattoexpect.com/pregnancy/checklist/hospital-packing.aspx

Geddes, J.K. (2021, May 10). *Hospital pre-registration for labor and delivery. What to Expect.* https://www.whattoexpect.com/pregnancy/labor-and-delivery/preparing/hospital-or-birthing-center.aspx

Gize, A., Eyassu, A., Nigatu, B. et al. *Men's knowledge and involvement on obstetric danger signs, birth preparedness, and complication readiness in Burayu town, Oromia region, Ethiopia. BMC Pregnancy Childbirth 19, 515 (2019).* https://doi.org/10.1186/s12884-019-2661-4

Gouza, M. (2022, August 10). *Fertility cliff myth: Exploring age, reproductive health, and fertility realities. Nutrisense.* https://www.nutrisense.io/blog/is-the-fertilitycliff-a-myth

Gurevich, R. (2022, November 29). *Why can't I get pregnant? 11 possible reasons. Very-well Family.* https://www.verywellfamily.com/why-cant-i-get-pregnant-if-imhealthy-1959936

Higuera, V. (2020, June 18). *7 things to consider when choosing a pediatrician. Health-line.* https://www.healthline.com/health/childrens-health/how-to-choose-apediatrician

Hoffmann, J. (2023, June 6). *The importance of self-care for dads. WilliamsburghChiropractic.* https://www.williamsburgchirony.com/blog/importance-selfcare-dads

Holland, K. (2023, March 10). 17 pregnancy do's and don'ts that may surprise you. Healthline. https://www.healthline.com/health/pregnancy/dos-and-donts

Holsey Stewart, D. (n.d.). 9 ways to make time for your partner after the baby arrives. Babycenter. https://www.babycenter.com/family/relationships/9-ways-tomake-time-for-your-partner-after-the-baby-arrives_365

Hope, A. (2024, February 4). Here's how platonic parenting works. Parents. https://www.parents.com/parenting/dynamics/how-platonic-parenting-works/

How to prepare your baby's nursery. (n.d.). SMA Nutrition. https://www.smababy.co.uk/pregnancy/nursery-preparation

Jacobson, J.D. (2022, April 19). Prenatal care in your third trimester. Medline Plus. https://medlineplus.gov/ency/patientinstructions/000558.htm

Jain, S. (2023, August 6). How often and how much should your baby eat? Healthy Children. https://www.healthychildren.org/English/ages-stages/baby/feeding-nutrition/Pages/how-often-and-how-much-should-your-baby-eat.aspx

Johnson, T.C. (2022, August 25). Choosing a health care provider for your pregnancy and childbirth. WebMD. https://www.webmd.com/baby/pregnancy-choosingobstetric-health-care-provider

Johnson, T.C. (2023, March 22). Second-trimester tests during pregnancy. WebMD. https://www.webmd.com/baby/second-trimester-tests

Johnson, T.C. (2023, March 22). First trimester tests during pregnancy. WebMD. https://www.webmd.com/baby/first-trimester-tests

Kam, K. (2023, June 9). *How often do I need prenatal visits?* WebMD. https://www.webmd.com/baby/how-often-do-i-need-prenatal-visits

Kashtan, P. (2023, May 30). *Your ultimate checklist of baby essentials. The Bump.* https://www.thebump.com/a/checklist-baby-essentials

Kashtan, P. (2024, January 19). *Hospital bag checklist: What to pack in hospital bag. The Bump.* https://www.thebump.com/a/checklist-packing-a-hospital-bag

Kelly, K. (2022, November 17). *10 labor and delivery support tips for partners. Parents.* https://www.parents.com/pregnancy/giving-birth/labor-support/labor-delivery-advice-dads/

Kennard, J. (2022, June 25). *A partner's guide to pregnancy in the third trimester. Very-well Family.* https://www.verywellfamily.com/pregnancy-guide-for-men-thethird-trimester-2328988

HealthPartners. (2021). *Labor signs and symptoms: What to expect as labor approaches and begins.* https://www.healthpartners.com/blog/labor-signs-and-symptoms/

LaBracio, J. (2023, December 6). *Ultimate hospital bag checklist for mom and baby. Babylist.* https://www.babylist.com/hello-baby/what-to-pack-in-your-hospitalbag

Lazic, M. (2023, May 20). *30+ divisive child custody statistics. Legal Jobs.* https://legaljobs.io/blog/child-custody-statistics

Livingston, G. & Parker, K. (2019, June 12). *8 facts about American dads. Pew Research Center.* https://www.pewresearch.org/short-reads/2019/06/12/fathers-day-facts/

LoMonaco, J.L. (2022). *How your body and brain change when you become a dad. Cradlewise.*

https://cradlewise.com/blog/how-fatherhood-changes-your-bodyand-brain

Making a birth plan. (2023, August). Pregnancy, Birth, and Baby. https://www.pregnancybirthbaby.org.au/making-a-birth-plan

March of Dimes. (2020, July). Newborn screening tests for your baby. https://www.marchofdimes.org/find-support/topics/parenthood/newborn-screening-testsyour-baby

March of Dimes. (2023a, September). Your body after baby: The first 6 weeks. https://www.marchofdimes.org/find-support/topics/postpartum/your-body-afterbaby-first-6-weeks

March of Dimes. (2023b, September). Your postpartum checkups. https://www.marchofdimes.org/find-support/topics/postpartum/your-postpartumcheckups

Masters, M. (2023a, January 6). 2-month-old baby. What to Expect. https://www.whattoexpect.com/first-year/month-by-month/month-2.aspx

Masters, M. (2023b, January 19). 3-month-old baby. What to Expect. https://www.whattoexpect.com/first-year/month-by-month/month-3.aspx

Masters, M. (2021, November 5). A partner's guide to life after childbirth. What to Expect. https://www.whattoexpect.com/pregnancy/for-dad/life-after-child birth.aspx

Mauer, E. (2019, December 3). A look at why relationships change after you have a baby. Healthline. https://www.healthline.com/health/parenting/relationshipchanges-after-baby

Mayo Clinic. (2022, December 23). Home pregnancy tests: Can you trust the results? https://www.mayoclinic.org/healthy-lifestyle/getting-pregnant/in-depth/home-pregnancy-tests/art-20047940

Mum's first few days after giving birth. (2021). Pregnancy, Birth, and Baby. https://www.pregnancybirthbaby.org.au/mums-first-few-days-after-giving-birth

Murray, D. (2023, August 16). How to choose a name for your baby? Parents. https://www.parents.com/baby-names-4014180

Nash, S.L. (2022, June 20). 9 questions to ask before deciding to have a baby. Psychcentral. https://psychcentral.com/lib/what-you-need-to-consider-before-havingkids

Nguyen, T.P. (2022, July). Prenatal tests: First trimester. Kids Health. https://kidshealth.org/en/parents/tests-first-trimester.html

Nguyen, T.P. (2022, July). Prenatal tests: Second trimester. Kids Health. https://kidshealth.org/en/parents/tests-second-trimester.html

Nguyen, T.P. (2022, July). Prenatal tests: Third trimester. Kids Health. https://kidshealth.org/en/parents/tests-third-trimester.html

Nuñez, A. (2022, April 19). How to find the best pediatrician for your baby. What to Expect. https://www.whattoexpect.com/pregnancy/checklist/potential-babydoctor.aspx

1-2 months: newborn development. (n.d.). Raising Children. https://raisingchildren.net.au/newborns/development/development-tracker/1-2-months

Parenthood and your relationship. (n.d.). Better Health. https://www.betterhealth.vic.gov.au/health/healthyliving/parenthood-and-your-relationship

Pathak, N. (2021, March 19). Second trimester tips. WebMD. https://www.webmd.com/baby/second-trimester-tips

Pregnancy - Signs and symptoms. (2022). Better Health Channel.

*https://www.betterhealth.vic.gov.au/health/healthyliving/pregna
ncy-signs-and-symptoms*

*Preparing your baby's room. (n.d.). Mustela.
https://www.mustelausa.com/blogs/mustela-mag/preparing-
your-baby-s-room*

*Risks of complication at every stage of pregnancy (n.d.). Birth
Injury Help Center.
https://www.birthinjuryhelpcenter.org/complication-
pregnant.html*

*Rockliffe, L. (2023, March 10). The importance of social
support in pregnancy and ways to connect with others.
Tommy's. https://www.tommys.org/pregnancy-
information/pregnancy-news-blogs/pregnancy-news-blogs-
being-pregnant/importance-social-support*

*Rodgers, L. (2022, June 13). Week-by-week pregnancy advice
for expecting dads and partners. What to Expect.
https://www.whattoexpect.com/pregnancy/for-dad/week-by-
week-pregnancy-advice-dads-partners/*

*Sample birth plan template. (2022, August). The American
College of Obstetricians and Gynecologists.
https://www.acog.org/womens-health/health-tools/sample-
birth-plan*

*Second trimester: 10 big things to think about for dads. (2017,
May). NCT. https://www.nct.org.uk/pregnancy/dads-be/second-
trimester-10-big-things-think-aboutfor-dads*

*Sheahan, K.P. (2019, September). Choosing a pediatrician for
your new baby. Kids health.
https://kidshealth.org/en/parents/find-ped.html*

*Sinrich, J. (2021, May 7). How to prepare for a baby
financially. What to Expect.
https://www.whattoexpect.com/pregnancy/checklist/finances.as
px*

*6 easy self-care tips for dads. (2023). Didofy.
https://didofy.com/parenting-advice/6-easy-self-care-tips-for-dads*

*Smith, L. (2018, June 27). Ten common labor complications. Medical News Today.
https://www.medicalnewstoday.com/articles/307462*

*Souza, K. (2019). Is platonic parenting or co-parenting for you? Keoni Souza Law.
https://www.keonisouzalaw.com/post/is-platonic-parenting-or-co-parentingfor-you*

*Stein, E., Gordon, S. & Riley, L. (2022, December 19). 9 signs labor is near: How to tell your baby will come soon. Parents.
https://www.parents.com/pregnancy/givingbirth/signs-of-labor/signs-of-approaching-labor/*

*Sullivan, D. (2020, April 20). The importance of checkups in the second trimester. Healthline.
https://www.healthline.com/health/pregnancy/second-trimestercheckups-tests*

*Sumner, C. & Scholsberg, S. (2023, January 4). 7 marriage problems after baby and how to solve them. Parents.
https://www.parents.com/parenting/relationships/staying-close/marriage-after-baby/*

*Terreri, C. (2017, June 5). To know or not to know your baby's sex - Pros & cons of finding out or keeping it secret. Lamaze.
https://www.lamaze.org/Giving-Birthwith-Confidence/GBWC-Post/to-know-or-not-to-know-your-babys-sexpros-cons-of-finding-out-or-keeping-it-secret*

*Tete, S. (2024, January 24). A complete guide on parental rights and responsibilities. Stylecraze.
https://www.stylecraze.com/articles/parental-rights-responsibilities/*

Treleaven, S. (2021, July 15). Why more people are having babies with their platonic friends. Today's Parent.

https://www.todaysparent.com/family/parenting/platonic-parenting-having-babies-with-friends/

Understanding your menstrual cycle. (2022, March 6). Tommy's. https://www.tommys.org/pregnancy-information/planning-a-pregnancy/how-to-get-pregnant/understanding-your-menstrual-cycle

Unplanned cesarean delivery. (n.d.). MoBap Baby. https://www.mobapbaby.org/Labor-Delivery/Types-of-Birth/Unplanned-Cesarean

Walsh, K. (2022, June 10). What to eat in the first trimester. What to Expect. https://www.whattoexpect.com/pregnancy/eating-well-menu/first-trimester.aspx

What to expect in the delivery room. (n.d.). Blue Kansas City. https://www.bluekc.com/resources/article/pregnancy/what-expect-delivery-room

Your baby's check-ups after they are born. (2021, March 25). Tommy's. https://www.tommys.org/pregnancy-information/after-birth/your-babys-check-ups-afterthey-are-born

Your pregnancy week by week. (2018) What to Expect. https://www.whattoexpect.com/pregnancy/week-by-week/

0-1 month: newborn development. (n.d.). Raising Children. https://raisingchildren.net.au/newborns/development/development-tracker/0-1-month

Zielger, A. (2022, April 12). Tips for successful co-parenting with a platonic friend. The Bump. https://www.thebump.com/a/platonic-co-parenting-tips

DAD, I'M COUNTING ON YOU!

How To Be A Hero In Your Baby's First 12 Months

By
Brad Wells

ISBN:

Printed in

First Edition, 2025

INTRODUCTION

There I was at 2:13 in the morning, a tiny baby staring up at me with big, blinking eyes. That's when I noticed my shirt was covered in spit-up. The baby had been hiccupping for two hours, and I was starting to wonder if that was normal. For the hundredth time that night, I hoped a secret manual was hidden somewhere in the house. Spoiler alert: there wasn't.

Once I was completely overwhelmed and exhausted, I realized that this is how the first 24 hours must be for most new dads. Prenatal classes and YouTube videos are great, but they don't prepare you for when the baby is actually in your living room. I know you want to be the hero your kid deserves and get everything right.

Those of you reading this are either in the middle of it, about to be in it, or still coming out of it. You might not feel like it yet, but you're a new dad. Maybe you feel like a guy in sweats with a baby tucked under one arm, unsure if you even brushed your teeth today. You're not alone, and you're not supposed to know everything. That's why I wrote this book.

This book is different. It won't tell you to just ask your partner or let mom handle it. This book is hands-on and practical. It will make you laugh when you need to. It's a survival guide for dads who want to be involved. It's for guys who want to jump in and get their hands dirty so they can be a dad their kid can look up to. Remember, it might take changing a diaper with one eye open at four in the morning.

I care because I've talked to hundreds of dads and read the research. I learned the difference between what works and what doesn't. I dedicated myself to helping first-time fathers. I have a passion for helping first-time fathers. I know it's easy to feel lost, left out. I want you to feel confident and included. I want you to take charge, no matter what life and your baby might throw at you.

How worried are you? Let's be honest, you're probably terrified of messing up. Are you worried that you can't calm down a screaming baby? Are you worried you'll say the wrong thing to your partner? So what if you're the only dad at daycare who can't fold a stroller? At this point, you're probably drowning in advice from all over. Trust me, you'll hear from family, friends, and even strangers in the diaper aisle. You might feel pressure to be the perfect dad, even if you have no idea what that really means.

Most parenting books aren't much help for dads. They're usually written with moms in mind. Some of the advice is so generic it could apply to raising a turtle. Others still lean on outdated stereotypes that don't reflect today's families. What you need is something different, something that speaks to you as a dad living in the modern world. That's what this book is all about.

Time to learn about "Dad Mode". I'm not making this up. It's a way of thinking that allows you to show up, learn fast, and not wait for permission. Dad Mode means you're in action, not on the sidelines. You take the shot knowing that you will miss sometimes.

This book is full of help you can use right now. You'll find checklists for every stage and dad hacks that actually work. You'll even get stories from dads who've been there. How would you like a month-by-month guide that walks you through the whole first year? Get real information on crying, sleep, bonding with your baby, and supporting your partner. Learn why swaddling isn't always the answer. This is a quick reference tool when you really need it.

Every kind of dad should see himself in these pages. Whether you're a single dad, part of a two-dad family, an adoptive dad, or a first-time dad at 45, this is for you. This book represents all dads and all kinds of families. You'll get real and practical advice even if your family is not like the ones you see on TV.

You might not believe it, especially if you've already tried other books full of fluff. But this one will give you the answers you need, fast. No filters, no sugarcoating. We'll get you through the night, the week, and your wild first year.

You can expect to have confidence from day one. You'll learn step-by-step skills in case you've never held a baby before. Learn to support your partner and take care of your own mental health. On top of that, you'll learn to balance work, money, and family. I'm giving you a roadmap for surviving while you enjoy these twelve beautiful and sometimes frustrating months.

I want you to get involved, not just read the pages. You can watch your baby grow by using the milestone tracker. Remember to fill out the 'Dad Win' pages and celebrate every victory. Start telling your stories. Join a community of new dads. I'm sure they're figuring it out one day, one diaper, and one bottle at a time.

I promise you're not alone and you're more capable than you think. Let this book be your go-to guide for the first year. This is Dad Mode. Your hero's journey starts now.

CHAPTER 1
Launching Dad Mode: Your First 24 Hours and Survival Week

Picture this: you walk in, baby carrier in one hand, hospital bag in the other, and your house suddenly feels foreign. The car seat still smells new. Your partner looks relieved but exhausted. You can't help thinking, "Who let me leave with a human?" It feels like someone in scrubs should chase you down and quiz you, but nobody does. Now, it's just you, your partner, and a tiny person making brand-new noises.

This is when Dad Mode begins. Not because you're ready, but because now you're the one to find answers. Most dads expect to feel prepared; few actually are. The first 24 hours are a blur of questions: how to hold, feed, and change your baby (a lot, by the way). You'll fuel yourself on adrenaline and pocket snacks.

The first week is overwhelming: cluster feeding (baby seems to eat non-stop), epic diaper blowouts, and emotions running high for both you and your partner. At 3 a.m., when you're exhausted and unsure, remember: nobody has it all together at first. This chapter is here to turn panic into purpose and give you a nitty-gritty playbook for those first days in Dad Mode.

Dad Mode On: Your 24-Hour Quick Start Plan

Here's what those first 24 hours at home look like. Keep things simple. Settle your baby into a safe sleep spot such as a crib, bassinet, or cot (hopefully already set up). Make sure diapers, wipes, onesies, and burp cloths are within reach. A snack and coffee station for parents is a lifesaver, especially for those bleary-eyed middle-of-the-night feedings.

Early on, you'll tackle your first diaper change. Lay out everything you need, such as wipes, fresh diaper, cream, and keep a hand on the baby to prevent escaping. Newborns are squirmy, and that first black-tar poop (meconium) is strange but normal. Don't stress about speed; you'll get quicker with practice (Diaper Changing Tips).

Then comes feeding. Babies eat often and unpredictably at first. Cluster feeding is when they eat almost hourly for hours; it's normal but exhausting. Be supportive if your partner is breastfeeding by offering snacks, water, and encouragement. If you're bottle feeding, having clean bottles ready saves time.

Take advantage of nap time, not just for the baby but for you and your partner too. Don't feel bad if you both zonk out on the couch while the baby sleeps in their safe space. It's survival, not slacking.

Fatigue reaches its peak by evening. The night shift is Dad Mode's proving ground: dim lights, quiet voices, and minimal stimulation help baby sort out day from night. Calm, quiet routines at night reassure your baby and your partner.

Emotions can surge after sunset. "Witching hour" fussiness is real, and so are the mood swings from both parents and the baby. Tears and frustration are normal.

Dad Mode isn't about always being confident; it's about pressing on even when you're uncertain. Your main job: tune in to your baby and partner, stay calm, and adapt when things go sideways.

Prepare a "baby zone" before you come home. Group essentials like diapers, wipes, onesies, and burp cloths together. Post emergency contacts where everyone will see them (fridge or charging station). Keep snacks and drinks within easy reach; nobody parents well when they're hangry.

Here's a dad hack: stash granola bars and water bottles in any area you might end up feeding or calming your baby during overnight shifts. Another: keep a notebook or whiteboard handy to jot down questions or reminders when you're half-awake.

Thoughts like "Is the baby breathing?" or "Was that noise normal?" are completely common and temporary. Every new dad has them.

If you find yourself joining "Team No Sleep," remember you're in good company. There are dads everywhere wandering around bleary-eyed, sipping cold coffee, and puzzling over baby gear.

Perfection isn't expected or required. Dad Mode is about showing up, again and again, even when you're exhausted, confused, or doubting yourself. That's what matters for your partner, for your baby, and for you.

The Essential "Don't Panic" Dad Checklist

Standing in your hallway after that hospital escape, you might freeze, unsure where to start. Newborns don't wait for you to get your bearings; they need food, clean butts, and a safe place to snooze. Everything else can wait. To keep the chaos from swallowing you, here's a straight-shooting checklist that gets you through the first night and week without losing your mind. Tape it to the fridge, screenshot it for your phone, or scrawl it on the back of a takeout menu. This is not about perfection, just keeping the basics rolling.

Dad Checklist: First Night and Week

- **Feeding Log:**

    - Mark each feeding (time, left/right if breastfeeding, or ounces if bottle).

o   Note spit-up, burps, and any "refusals."

o   Track diapers after feeds; pee and poop both count.

- **Diaper Station Setup:**

  o   Stash at least 10-12 diapers within arm's reach.

  o   Wipes (open package before baby arrives, trust me).

  o   Diaper cream/tube handy for red butts.

  o   Two backup onesies because accidents happen in streaks.

  o   Spare plastic bags or a diaper pail for the stink bombs.

- **Partner Wellness Check:**

  o   Ask directly: "How are you feeling?" and mean it.

  o   Offer snacks, water, or a break.

  o   Keep any necessary meds, pads, or supports close for easy access.

  o   Remind them they're not alone in this.

- **Sleep Setup:**

o Baby's crib or bassinet should be clear of toys, pillows, and blankets, with just a fitted sheet.

o Nightlight for low-key check-ins.

o Your own pillow/blanket nearby for crash-landings between shifts.

Here's the real secret: don't waste your nerves on things that simply don't matter this week. That pile of laundry? Ignore it unless you've run out of burp cloths. Forget about deep cleaning the kitchen or alphabetizing the freezer. Elaborate baby schedules are pointless in week one; your newborn is running the show, and the script changes every hour. Grocery trips can wait unless you're out of diapers, wipes, or coffee.

New dads get tripped up by panic points that seem like emergencies but usually aren't. Non-stop crying will make your heart race, but babies cry for reasons as simple as being tired, hungry, overstimulated, or needing a fresh diaper. If the checklist isn't solving it, try:

- Check diaper (sometimes it's just wet).

- Offer food even if they just ate. Cluster feeding is real.

- Burp your baby with gentle pats on the back while supporting their head.

- Walk around holding your baby upright (gravity helps with gas).

- Dim the lights and lower the noise; sometimes babies just want calm.

If spit-up happens, and it will, don't stress unless it's projectile or green or yellow every time. Most newborns spit up after feeds because their digestive systems are still learning the ropes. Wipe baby down, swap outfits if needed, and keep burp cloths close.

If your baby won't latch while breastfeeding, try skin-to-skin contact for a few minutes, gently tickle their cheek to encourage rooting, and stay calm because babies pick up on stress fast. If you're bottle feeding and they refuse, check the temperature or try a different nipple size.

Blowout Protocol: When you open a diaper and find a situation that looks like a crime scene, don't panic. Lay everything out before you begin. Use wipes liberally; there's no prize for thriftiness in this battle. Roll up the old diaper underneath the baby as you work, so you have a clean landing zone. If things go sideways, literally, just breathe and remember that every dad has been christened by a blowout at least once.

Knowing what not to worry about will save your sanity. Don't obsess over whether your baby is sleeping "enough." Newborns sleep in strange patterns; charts and averages don't matter yet. Don't compare your baby (or yourself) to anyone else on social media because filters hide the messier truth. Most importantly, don't beat yourself up if things feel clumsy or awkward; all new dads start out that way.

Some newborn quirks are totally normal: hiccups that last forever, sneezing fits, jerky arm movements, noisy breathing (as long as there's no blue coloring or struggling for air). Red flags that do need quick action include fever over 100.4°F (38°C), refusal to eat for more than two feeds in a row, blue lips or skin, trouble breathing (not just noisy), or limpness that doesn't improve when awake. Call your pediatrician right away if you spot any of these.

Dad Wins Reflection Box

Jot down the small stuff that went right each day, even if it's as simple as "got baby to sleep without drama" or "kept my cool during a meltdown." These tiny wins are proof: you're getting better at this every hour. They'll keep you going when fatigue wants to take over and doubt creeps in.

Tag-Teaming: How to Rock the First Night with Your Partner

That first night at home, you and your partner are running on excitement, nerves, and maybe a little caffeine. Suddenly, reality hits: this tiny human needs care around the clock, and there's no shift change coming. Here's where true tag-teaming begins. Forget the idea that one parent is "better" or should do more; this is a partnership, not a contest.

Divide and conquer is your new mantra. You hand off the baby like a football after a feed, or swap places at the changing table, so nobody gets stuck with the same job all night. If you're prepping bottles, one of you can wash and fill while the other does a quick diaper check or rocks the baby. When the baby cries for the third time in an hour, calling out, "Your turn for baby jail duty!" can break the tension and get you both laughing instead of arguing.

Setting up a routine from the start, maybe alternating feeds or taking turns on diaper duty, keeps resentment at bay and gives each of you brief but necessary breaks.

Communication becomes survival gear, not just a nice idea. When one of you is fading fast or patience is thin, clear signals are vital. A simple "I need five minutes" or "Can you take over?" is often all it takes to prevent a meltdown, yours or the baby's. Sometimes, you just need a break to step outside or splash cold water on your face. Having code words or gestures helps too. Maybe it's a thumbs up for "I'm good" or a hand on the shoulder for "I'm about to lose it." Don't be afraid to say what you need; mind-reading doesn't work at 3 a.m.

Scripts help when words are hard to find in the fog of sleep deprivation. Try these: "What do you need right now?" opens the door for honesty without blame. "Want me to take over for a bit?"

shows empathy and teamwork. Or keep it light with, "You do diapers, I'll handle negotiations with our tiny dictator." Humor diffuses tension better than any deep breath app. Even just saying, "We're doing our best" out loud can settle nerves and remind you both that nobody gets graded on style points tonight.

Resentment grows when one person feels they're carrying too much. Maybe you catch yourself thinking, "Why am I always doing this?" It happens to everyone, even with the best intentions. The myth that moms have some secret code for babies leads to dads feeling sidelined or clueless. This isn't true; skills come from practice, not chromosomes.

I've heard from dads who felt like background extras in their own homes until they started taking nighttime shifts or bottle feeds. One dad I know told me he never felt like a real parent until he took over every other night so his partner could sleep; by week two, he knew his baby's different cries and started volunteering for the night shift. Another dad shared that he and his husband rotated roles every feeding, one did the bottle, the other changed diapers, so nobody felt stuck or left out.

Quick nightly check-ins work wonders. After the baby finally nods off (even if it's only for 23 minutes), sit together for five minutes and ask: "What worked tonight? What should we tweak tomorrow?" These huddles aren't about blame; they're your chance to adjust game plans as a team. Maybe you realize that swapping jobs every two hours helps both of you stay sane, or that prepping bottles before bed means less stumbling around in the dark at midnight. Celebrate any win, no matter how small, before crashing for some rest. A high-five, fist bump, or even just a whispered "We survived!" cements your teamwork.

Starting a "parent win" ritual can become something you look forward to each day. Maybe you share one thing that went well, like "I kept my cool during the meltdown," "You got her to burp in record time," "We didn't argue about whose turn it was." Little victories matter more than perfect routines.

Tag-teaming isn't always smooth; sometimes miscommunication happens, tempers flare, or one person feels invisible. Don't let those moments define your partnership. Reset as needed, step back in, apologize quickly if needed, and move forward knowing every team has rough nights. The goal isn't perfect harmony; it's having each other's backs when things get loud and messy.

If you ever feel frustration rising, remember: this is not about keeping score. It's about surviving together and sharing both the chaos and the quiet moments. Nobody keeps track of who did more; what matters is nobody feels alone doing it all. The first night sets the tone for many more ahead; working together now builds habits that will help you both down the road.

Baby's First Diaper: A No-Fear, No-Mess Guide

Changing your baby's diaper for the first time feels like being handed a bomb you're supposed to disarm while blindfolded. Your palms sweat, your mind races, and you wonder why nobody mentioned the weird stickiness of that first poop. The trick is to slow down and break the process into steps.

First, set up your changing station before you even open the diaper. Line up wipes, a clean diaper, a thin layer of diaper cream, and an extra onesie because leaks happen when you least expect them. Place your baby on a flat, stable surface (changing table, bed with a towel, or even the floor if you're desperate), and always keep one hand steady on your baby. Babies are wriggly, and they have a knack for rolling at the worst moments.

Open the dirty diaper slowly, pausing for any surprise sprays; little boys are notorious for launching a stream at inopportune times. Wipe gently from front to back for girls to prevent infection. Lift your baby's legs by the ankles with your free hand and slide the new diaper underneath before removing the old one, so you're ready if there's a last-minute eruption. Use wipes liberally, don't skimp, and immediately roll up the soiled diaper and wipes into a tight ball, sealing it before tossing it out.

Blowouts are their own beast. You'll know one when you see it: poop up the back, down the legs, maybe even in the hair. Stay calm. Strip baby down, wipe from top to bottom, and use as many wipes as necessary. If things get truly out of hand, run a warm washcloth or even give a quick bath. It's not about staying clean; it's about keeping your cool when chaos hits. Laugh if you can; one day this will be a story you tell at their wedding.

Odd colors like green or orange can pop up depending on what your partner eats while breastfeeding or from harmless bile changes. What matters more than color is how your baby seems—happy, eating well, no fever? You're good. Only worry if you see red (blood), chalky white (possible liver issue), or black after the first few days. In that case, call your pediatrician.

Speed and organization make diapers less stressful. A "dad hack" I swear by: set up multiple diaper caddies around the house; in the living room, bedroom, and car trunk with all the basics so you're never sprinting upstairs mid-meltdown. Keep plastic bags for dirty diapers handy in each spot. Practice pulling wipes out with one hand (trust me, you'll need that skill at 3 a.m.), and pre-open wipe packs so you're not fumbling with sticky tabs mid-change.

Worrying about hurting your baby or messing up is common; every dad I know has had those nerves at first. Babies are tougher than they look, but go gentle. Support their head and neck with your non-dominant hand when lifting legs; avoid yanking or twisting limbs. If you're nervous about cleaning sensitive spots or applying cream, go slow and talk to your baby as you work, even if they don't understand yet, your voice will calm both of you.

You will mess up sometimes. Maybe you stick the tabs wrong and have to start over while your baby pees on the clean diaper. Maybe you get poop on your own shirt (or worse). Everybody fumbles their first changes. One night I tried to wrestle a onesie over my daughter's head mid-blowout and somehow managed to get poop on my ear. Instead of panicking or feeling defeated, I just laughed. What else can you do? These mistakes don't make you a bad dad; they make you human.

The more you change diapers, the faster and more confident you'll become. Every time you succeed, no matter how clumsy it feels, you're building skills that matter. Tell yourself after each change: "I did it." You'll get quicker, cleaner, and less rattled each time until it's just another part of the day, like making coffee or tying your shoes.

Safely Handling and Soothing Your Newborn (Without Swaddling)

At first, handling your baby can make your arms feel too big and your hands unsure, but confidence develops quickly. Always move slowly, keeping one hand under your baby's head and neck, and the other supporting their bottom. Hold your baby close to your chest for comfort and stability. When picking up or putting down your baby, whether from a crib or changing table, slide a forearm behind their neck and upper back, scoop under their bottom with your other hand, and bring them close for warmth and calm.

The football hold is popular, especially for dads: place your baby along your forearm, body against your side, head in your palm facing out, legs behind. This provides great feeding support and lets you keep a hand free for multitasking. For soothing, the cross-body hold often works well—baby belly-down across both arms, head nuzzled in your elbow, feet over the opposite arm. When burping, drape the baby on your chest with their chin on your shoulder, or sit them upright on your lap; support the chest and head with one hand and gently tap their back with the other.

Swaddling was once a rite of passage, but now carries risks if not done just right. Babies who roll or are swaddled too loosely may get tangled, which isn't safe for sleep. The American Academy of Pediatrics now advises stopping swaddling once your baby shows signs of rolling. Alternatives like wearable sleep sacks with arm holes keep babies cozy but unrestricted. For calming before sleep, use other techniques: shushing near their ear (mimicking womb sounds), gentle rocking, and white noise machines or apps to mask distractions. Many newborns find comfort in a clean pacifier, though never force it.

Learning your newborn's cries is like cracking a secret code. With time, patterns become clear. A hungry cry builds up gradually, including "neh" sounds and rooting or sucking cues. Tired cries are rhythmic and whiny; look for red eyelids or yawns. Gas pain comes with sharp, short cries, knees pulled up, and a tense face. Overstimulation leads to high-pitched cries, flailing arms, and avoiding light or noise. Fast responses help: offer food for hunger cues, swaddle-free snuggle or rocking for tiredness, gentle tummy massages or bicycle legs for gas.

Swaddle fails are common; babies wriggle free, blankets slip, and anxieties rise. One of my first attempts ended with my daughter escaping both arms and feet in seconds. After that, I switched to a sleep sack and focused on her needs: my hand on her chest, soft humming, dim lights. Sleep sacks became the default; they kept her both warm and safe.

Most new dads have a story about botched swaddles, blankets on faces, and late-night panics. The breakthrough happens when you watch your baby's cues instead of sticking to strict routines. Sometimes soothing is just holding her upright, walking in a dim room, and whispering. Other times, it's a combination: pacifier, white noise, gentle sway, whatever works in the moment.

Every baby is different. Some like side-to-side rocking, others want to bounce gently on a yoga ball, regardless of your singing abilities. Try various holds and moves until you see what calms your baby. If it takes three techniques in five minutes to settle things down, that's normal. Parenting is about adapting, building confidence, and remembering that genuine connection matters more than perfect technique.

Quick Cry Decoder (Reference)

- **Hungry**: Rhythmic "neh" cries and rooting, offer food.

- **Tired**: Whimpers, eye rubbing, yawns, try rocking or gentle soothing.

- **Gassy**: Short, bursty cries with knees up, try burping or tummy massage.

- **Overstimulated**: High-pitched cries, turning away, move to a dark, quiet room, try soft shushing.

Trust yourself; you'll read these signals faster each day, and your handling will feel more natural. Your baby will feel your confidence grow. When nothing works, simply hold your baby close and breathe together until calm returns.

Real-World Dad Scenarios: Troubleshooting the First 48 Hours

Picture yourself slumped on the edge of the bed at 2 a.m., baby wailing so loud it rattles the window. You've tried rocking, feeding, checked the diaper, and even resorted to whispering a sports play-by-play just to fill the silence between cries. Nothing works. This is that "choose your own adventure" moment: do you freeze, tag in your partner, or run through a mental checklist? Most dads hit this wall early; what matters is how you move through it.

First, breathe (inhale for four, exhale for six). Scan for obvious issues: diaper (wet or dry?), hunger (last meal time?), gas (knees up, little tummy rub). If none of those click, try changing the scenery. Walk the hallway with the lights low, or head to the bathroom where the sound of running water hums in the background. Some babies just need a shift.

If that doesn't soothe, skin-to-skin contact often does wonders. If your baby's still inconsolable for more than two hours or shows signs of illness (fever, limpness, bluish color), call your pediatrician. Trust your gut, not just Google.

Decision trees can keep your mind steady when panic wants to take over. For endless crying:

- Start with comfort checks (diaper, feeding, burp).

- Next, try movement (rock, sway, walk).

- Then offer a pacifier or a gentle shushing sound.

- If nothing changes and your baby seems distressed (not just fussy), check for fever or odd breathing.

- Still worried? Make the call; no shame in asking for help.

Now, every dad has a confession. One night, I spent fifteen minutes hunting for a pacifier only to find it stuck to my sock. Another time, in a foggy haze, I put my baby's onesie on backward and only noticed when her feet poked out the neck hole. One dad I know panicked when his daughter sneezed fifteen times in a row, convinced she had some rare disease, when all she needed was a little nose suction and a cuddle. These mistakes aren't failures; they're proof you care enough to worry. Laugh at them when you can. Parenthood's hard enough without adding guilt.

For those moments when things feel less funny and more frightening, quick "What Now?" guides can be lifesavers. Let's talk emergencies that spike every dad's heart rate:

- **Choking:** If your baby suddenly can't cry or cough and looks panicked or turns blue, act fast. Turn her face down on your forearm, support her head, and give five firm pats between her shoulder blades with the heel of your hand. If she's still struggling, turn her face up and give five gentle chest compressions with two fingers just below the nipple line. Alternate until she coughs or help arrives. Call 911 right away if she doesn't respond.

- **Fever:** A rectal temperature over 100.4°F (38°C) in a newborn is an emergency. Call your pediatrician or head to the ER immediately. Don't wait it out; newborns can get sick fast.

- **Partner in Distress:** Sometimes the one who needs urgent help isn't the baby, it's your partner. Watch for signs of emotional overload: crying spells that don't stop, withdrawing from you or the baby, anger that feels out of character, or talk of hopelessness. Offer comfort and ask directly if they feel safe. If you sense it's more than exhaustion, reach out to their OB or a support line, even strong parents need backup.

Mistakes will come thick and fast in these first days, but so will victories. Maybe you finally calmed your baby after an hour-long meltdown or figured out how to change a diaper without needing a fresh shirt yourself. Perhaps you let your partner sleep an extra hour while you walked laps with your newborn pressed against your chest. Small wins like these add up. They matter more than any flawless routine. High five yourself each time you make it through a tough moment.

Here's what many new dads miss: showing up matters more than getting everything right. The wins are real, even if they're small, like holding your ground through a crying fit or making your partner laugh when both of you are running on empty. Each day you stick around, learn from mistakes, and keep going is proof that you're exactly the dad your kid needs: present, caring, and real.

CHAPTER 2
Mastering the Fundamentals: Hands-On Baby Care for Dads

The Ultimate Bottle and Breastfeeding Support Guide for Dads

Imagine it's late at night: your baby's hungry, you're bleary-eyed, and the bottle warmer looks like a puzzle. Bottle and breastfeeding might seem daunting, but dads are essential to both. No matter how your baby eats, bottle, breast, or both, your support, patience, and hands-on help are invaluable.

For bottle feeds, formula, pumped milk, or both, set up a routine to make things easy when you're tired. Prep bottles by following the formula's directions precisely; even a small measurement mistake can upset your baby's stomach. Fill bottles with fresh (preferably filtered) water, add powder, shake well, and ensure lids and nipples are secure to avoid spills. Label pumped breast milk bottles clearly with the date and time. They can be kept at room temperature for up to four hours, in the fridge for up to four days, or in the freezer for up to six months. Never heat bottles in the microwave; use a bowl of warm water or a bottle warmer, and swirl gently to mix.

A dedicated "bottle station" makes a big difference. Use a section of the kitchen or a cart for bottles, nipples, formula, and burp cloths. Having extra bottles on hand saves stress on busy days. Prep for nighttime by filling bottles with water and pre-measuring scoops of formula. For twins or combo feeding, color-code or use different-shaped bottles.

If your partner breastfeeds, your role is crucial, besides producing milk! Take charge of burping: keep a cloth handy and gently pat your baby's back. Help by arranging pillows or adjusting seating for comfort. "Water and cookie runs" are classics for dads: bring snacks and drinks during long feeds. Offer encouragement over advice. Try "You're doing an amazing job" or "How can I help?" without switching to problem-solving unless asked. If your partner needs to vent, just listen and be present; sometimes sitting beside her is the best support.

For combo feeding, pace bottle feeds: hold the bottle horizontally so baby has to suck at the same pace as breastfeeding, which helps avoid confusion. Switch up who gives bottles so both parents get bonding time and rest. Many families use slow-flow nipples for a smoother transition. Test different brands if your baby fusses or rejects a bottle, as some have strong preferences.

Dads often spot feeding troubles early. Signs of a poor latch during breastfeeding include smacking sounds, lips curled inward, lots of dribbling, or pain for your partner. If you notice any of these, suggest a pause and help reposition the baby. With bottles, refusal can mean the milk is flowing too fast or too slow. Gassy babies clench their fists, arch their backs, and pull up their knees. Pace the feeds and burp often to help.

Spit-up and fussiness are common. If your baby spits up but seems content and gains weight, just keep burp cloths handy. If spit-up is forceful, greenish, or accompanied by pain or poor feeding, call your pediatrician. For fussiness, check that bottles are the right temperature, try feeding upright, or offer smaller, more frequent bottles.

Here are simple "dad hacks":

- Use dishwasher baskets so bottle parts don't vanish.

- Keep a stash of clean bottles in the fridge.

- Set phone alarms for using or freezing pumped milk.

- Gather all night-time feeding supplies before bed.

- Place burp cloths everywhere: car, couch, and changing table.

Emotional support matters as much as practical help. Feeding can bring frustration and guilt. Don't suggest formula unless your partner does; instead, say something like, "I see how hard you're working." If things get tough, remind each other you're a team and that a fed baby is what matters.

Reflection Exercise: Feeding Wins and Lessons

After each feed, jot down what worked (like a bottle your baby accepted) or a supportive word that mattered. These notes become a toolkit of what works for your family and proof that you're mastering this, one feed at a time.

Burping Without the Barf: Dad-Tested Techniques

Burping your baby is one of those rituals that quickly becomes second nature, but it can feel awkward and a little nerve-wracking at first. You'll probably find yourself cycling through different positions, trying to find the one that works best for your baby.

Over-the-shoulder is the classic move. Drape a burp cloth across your shoulder (and maybe down your back for extra coverage), then hold your baby upright with their chin resting just above your collarbone. Use one hand to support their bottom and the other to gently pat or rub their back in slow circles. This position is a favorite for a reason. It's easy, lets gravity do some of the work, and usually gets a solid burp out in record time. The downside? If your baby's going to spit up, your shirt might be collateral damage.

The sitting-on-lap method comes in handy when your back needs a break. Sit your baby on your knee facing away from you, support their chest and head with one hand (forming a "C" with your fingers under their chin), and use the other hand to pat or rub their back. This position gives you a clear view of your baby's face, so you can spot any warning signs of an impending spit-up attack.

For gassy babies who need extra help, try the face-down-on-knees trick. Lay your baby belly-down across your knees, head slightly higher than their chest, and pat or rub gently. Sometimes that change in pressure helps stubborn air bubbles escape.

Babies give plenty of hints when they need to burp; you just have to watch for them. If your little one squirms, arches their back, draws their knees up, or suddenly stops feeding and looks annoyed, there's probably a burp hiding in there. Fussiness during feeds, clenched fists, or grimacing faces are other signs it's time for a quick burp break. With bottle-fed babies, try to pause every couple of ounces to get those bubbles out before they build up. Breastfed babies may need a burp after each breast or whenever they unlatch.

Sometimes burps play hard to get. If you're patting and nothing happens after a couple of minutes, switch up the position; gravity can be your best friend. Some babies respond better to gentle rubs in a circular motion rather than firm pats. Others prefer a combination, light tapping followed by a slow upward stroke along the spine. If your baby falls asleep before you get a burp, don't panic; not every feed ends with a belch. Never force it. If your baby is relaxed and not showing signs of discomfort, it's okay to let it go.

Spit-up is almost inevitable, especially in the early weeks. When it happens, keep calm and reach for that burp cloth you wisely placed within arm's reach. Quick swaps are key. A clean cloth over your shoulder and another within grabbing distance for your baby's face or clothes can save you from needing an outfit change yourself. For especially messy spit-ups, keep an emergency onesie tucked behind the couch or in your diaper caddy for rapid response.

Dad hacks for containing the chaos? Place burp cloths everywhere: on chairs, couches, even across your lap if you're feeding in bed. Tuck an extra shirt for yourself into the diaper bag or stash one in the car for post-spit-up emergencies. During night feeds, have a "burp station" with spare cloths, wipes, and pajamas close by. You'll thank yourself when disaster strikes at 2 a.m. For quick cleanups, keep baby wipes within reach, not just for them but for you too. There's nothing like realizing you've been walking around with dried milk on your neck all day.

Normalize the mess; it's part of the new dad experience. The first time my daughter unleashed a full-on spit-up that ran down my back and pooled in my shoe, I thought I'd failed some kind of parenting test. Turns out, it happens to everyone.

One dad friend confessed he once caught spit-up in his bare hands just to save his new couch. Another dad remembered patting so vigorously during his rookie week that he ended up with a gassy but still very un-burped baby and an angry partner who'd just changed her shirt for the third time that morning.

My favorite "burp fail" happened when I tried to multitask on a work call while burping my son. He managed to spit up on both my shirt and my laptop keyboard, forcing me to finish the meeting in a bathrobe.

You'll develop "dad reflexes" faster than you think, like catching spit-up midair or swapping out a onesie in under twenty seconds flat. The key is not taking any of this too seriously; every dad has stories of disasters narrowly avoided or epic fails survived, with only minor stains as proof. Laugh off the goofs, celebrate the wins (even if they're tiny), and know that every mess cleaned up is another notch on your dad belt. The more relaxed you are about burping and its aftermath, the more confident you'll become. And trust me, your baby will pick up on that calm.

Bath Time Basics: Safety, Fun, and Dad Wins

Bathing your newborn for the first time can feel nerve-wracking. Newborns are tiny, wiggly, and can startle you with sudden cries. You might imagine peaceful bubbles, but usually, it's more like a water experiment. If you're anxious, you're not alone; many new dads worry about dropping the baby or making a mess. The important thing is: newborns do not need daily baths. Three times a week is enough, and more can dry out their skin. Until the umbilical stump falls off (usually in the first week or so), stick to sponge baths. Choose a warm, draft-free spot, like the kitchen counter, changing table, or a bed with a towel.

Gather everything beforehand: two towels, a soft washcloth, a little rinsing cup, mild baby soap, a fresh diaper, and clean clothes. Fill a basin or bowl with warm (not hot) water and check with your elbow. It should feel comfortably warm, never hot.

Lay your baby on the towel and keep most of them wrapped, exposing only one limb at a time. Wet the washcloth and start with the cleanest parts: face, then neck folds (where milk often hides), armpits, hands, and legs. Clean the diaper area last to avoid spreading germs. Use only a little soap for the scalp or hair; newborns don't get very dirty. Never leave your baby alone, even for a second. Talking or singing calms both of you; narrate what you're doing or hum a tune. Don't stress about getting it "right"; just focus on making your baby feel safe.

When you move to tub baths after the cord stump falls off, keep things simple. Use a small tub with a non-slip bottom in the sink or bathtub, and add two or three inches of warm water. Double-check the temperature with your wrist or elbow before you start. Hold your baby's head and neck with one arm and wash with the other. Some babies love the water, some will cry, but don't panic. Just stay calm and try to be quick yet gentle.

A common concern is how slippery wet babies can be. Keep a hand under their armpit and across their chest wherever possible. Have everything within reach: shampoo, soft cradle cap brush, and towels. To prevent water in the ears, gently tilt their head or use a damp washcloth rather than pouring water. Tears are normal at first, especially if your baby is hungry or tired. Move efficiently, then wrap your baby in a hooded towel and snuggle them dry.

Bath time accidents are normal. Expect some splashing or the classic surprise pee mid-bath. You might drop the soap or fumble a towel. Stay light-hearted; every dad goes through these moments. Soon, you'll figure out what works best. Maybe soft background music or letting your baby hold a little washcloth helps them relax.

Bath time isn't just about cleaning, it's prime dad-bonding time. The first time I bathed my son solo, he screamed as soon as his foot touched water. I started singing "Rubber Duckie," and to my relief, he paused, letting me finish. I snapped a selfie afterward as proof I survived. If you want to mark these moments, take a photo, calm or not; a wild hair shot is priceless. Make a ritual with a regular song or silly saying; over time, your child will expect it and may even laugh.

As your baby grows, a soft bath toy or rubber duck can distract them. Keep baths brief; five to ten minutes is enough. Dry well between skin folds to prevent irritation. Celebrate little milestones, like the first splash or the first time your baby reaches for the water.

Bathing your baby isn't about perfection; it's about patience and care as you learn together. Every bath builds your confidence and your baby's trust. Those are the real wins.

Diaper Blowouts: Prevention, Cleanup, and Staying Cool

Diaper blowouts are a common, humbling part of parenting, especially in the early weeks when babies are on liquid diets and their digestive systems are unpredictable. Many think blowouts are just bad luck, but in reality, proper fit and timing matter a lot. If a diaper is too loose at the legs or too small for your baby's growing belly, leaks are inevitable.

To make sure the fit is right, check the snugness at the waist (below the belly button), look for no gaping at the thighs, and make sure the tabs are evenly fastened. Red marks mean it's too tight; gaps or sagging mean it's too big. Always size by weight, not age, and refer to the manufacturer's guide on the diaper pack. Sometimes a particular brand just won't suit your baby's shape, so don't hesitate to try a few before settling on the right one.

When a blowout happens, and it will eventually, your mission is to keep the mess from spreading. The key tool is the "blowout kit": pack a couple of diapers, travel wipes, a soft cloth, a change of clothes for the baby (and maybe for yourself), and two plastic bags (one for dirty items, one for used wipes and diapers). Keep a kit everywhere you might need it: in the diaper bag, car, stroller, and by your main changing area at home.

When you spot a blowout, like stains creeping up the back or down the legs, act quickly. Lay your baby on a wipeable surface (avoid soft furnishings), roll the onesie down using the shoulder "envelopes" to avoid getting the mess in their hair, and use plenty of wipes or give a quick rinse in the tub if needed. Seal dirty clothes and diapers in a bag, take a deep breath, and remind yourself you handled it like a pro.

Preparation and speed are crucial. Keep old towels or puppy pads handy for backup changing surfaces. If a blowout hits furniture, blot with wipes, then use a safe disinfectant spray. Avoid scrubbing to prevent deep stains. In public, use family bathrooms when you can, or turn your car's trunk into a makeshift changing area. If needed, open both rear doors on your car for some privacy. Never change a baby on restaurant tables; people remember that move.

Nighttime blowouts are especially tough when you're tired and slow to react. Having pajamas and wipes within reach makes things easier. Some use double-diapering at night (a larger diaper over the normal one) if their baby is especially prone to leaks.

Dad strategies make a huge difference when you're facing blowouts. Pre-pack several diaper bags: keep one in the car, one by the door, and one attached to the stroller. Always include at least two changes of baby clothes (one won't cut it), and maybe a spare shirt for yourself. For public incidents, create a "containment zone" with extra mats or disposable liners. If things go south, just get the job done, protect your dignity, and move on with a sense of humor.

Most dads have a blowout horror story. For some, it's the back-and-leg coverage at a picnic; for others, it's a 3 a.m. mess where they wear as much as the baby. The truth is, no one gets it right every time, but you get faster and calmer with each one. After a few blowouts, you become unfazed. Grab your kit, protect the surroundings, and act.

Ultimately, what matters isn't your cleaning speed or stain removal skills, but your attitude when things go wrong. Embarrassment vanishes when you realize it's a universal dad experience. Laugh at yourself, forget about ruined clothes, and push ahead. Blowouts remind you that, despite the chaos, your presence and willingness to handle the mess are most important, even if you smell like wipes and baby powder afterwards.

Safe Sleep Without Swaddling: What Works Now

The rules for safe baby sleep have changed a lot over the years, and if you're like me, you probably heard all sorts of advice from grandparents, friends, or even your own parents about wrapping your baby up tight. But here's the honest truth: swaddling isn't considered the go-to answer anymore. The main reason is safety. Once babies get strong enough to roll, even a little, a swaddle can become a hazard if it slips or the baby ends up face down. The

American Academy of Pediatrics now recommends ditching swaddles as soon as your baby shows any signs of rolling over. Instead, you want your baby to sleep on their back, always, on a firm mattress with a fitted sheet only. No bumpers, pillows, stuffed animals, or loose blankets in the crib. It might look a little bare, but that's exactly how it should be. Minimal is best for safe sleep.

So what do you do when your baby startles awake or fusses without that tight swaddle? Enter the hero of modern sleep: the sleep sack. These wearable blankets keep babies warm without any loose fabric in the crib. There are tons of options; some with arms out, some with gentle snugness around the torso but freedom for the legs. Layer your baby in a onesie and footed pajamas under the sleep sack for chilly nights. If you're worried about them getting cold, remember: one more layer than you're wearing is usually plenty.

White noise machines can work wonders too. Steady sounds help block out household noise and mimic the whoosh babies heard in the womb. Place the machine near the crib but away from your baby's head, and keep it at a low volume. Pacifiers are also recommended for safe sleep after breastfeeding is established; they can soothe and reduce the risk of SIDS.

A pre-sleep routine is gold for signaling "bedtime" to your baby's little brain. This doesn't have to be complicated. Dim the lights, put on soft music or white noise, and move slowly through diaper changes and pajamas. A gentle rocking session or soft singing can help your baby wind down. Try the same steps each night; babies catch on quickly when there's a predictable pattern. You'll notice them yawning or rubbing their eyes when they sense bedtime coming.

Even with all these tools, you'll probably run into challenges like startle reflexes; those sudden flailing arms that wake your baby just as you tiptoe out of the room. Startle reflex is normal and fades with age, but it can be tough in those early weeks. Sleep sacks with snug upper bodies help keep arms in check without restricting movement dangerously. Layering for warmth is another trick; sometimes a well-fitted onesie and cozy sack can make your baby feel secure enough to settle back down.

If your baby wakes often or fights sleep, try holding them upright and gently rocking side to side, not up and down, for a few minutes before putting them back down drowsy but awake.

Night wakings are part of the deal, especially early on, but there are ways to make them less brutal. Tag-team with your partner if possible; split shifts or alternate who gets up each time so neither of you burns out completely. If you're solo, set up everything you might need (diapers, wipes, bottle/supplies) within arm's reach of the crib before you go to bed. Keep lights low during wake-ups so your baby knows it's still "sleep time," not playtime.

Tracking your baby's sleep doesn't have to be complicated; a simple log helps spot patterns and celebrate progress. Use a notebook or a phone app to jot down when your baby goes down and wakes up, plus notes on what helped (or didn't). You'll start to see trends: maybe she does longer stretches after a warm bath or fusses less with white noise on. It's so easy to miss progress when you're exhausted, but looking back at your notes and seeing "first three-hour stretch!" or "self-soothed at 2 a.m." can give you a boost when you need it most.

Those small victories, when your baby sleeps through a diaper change without waking fully, or finally soothes herself with a pacifier, are wins worth celebrating. Maybe you get an extra hour of shut-eye, or you high-five your partner at 5 a.m. after surviving another night shift. These moments add up; each one builds confidence and proves you're figuring this out together, one night at a time.

Sleep Log Template

Just jot this in your phone notes or on a sticky by the crib:

- Down time:

- Wake time:

- How long they slept:

- What helped them settle:

- Any "win" (like longer stretch or less fuss): Seeing those wins, even tiny ones, reminds you this stage won't last forever, and you're doing better than you think.

Taming the Witching Hour: Soothing Strategies for Fussy Evenings

Every new dad gets hit with the "witching hour" at some point, and it's a wild ride. Picture this: the sun's gone down, you're wiped, and suddenly your calm baby turns into a tiny, red-faced siren. Usually, this madness kicks off between five and eight in the evening. It's almost like your baby's internal alarm clock is set to "maximum chaos" right when you're hoping for a breather.

If you're staring at your child, wondering why nothing calms them, you're in good company. This is the time of day when babies often get overstimulated, overtired, or just plain cranky from all the new sights and sounds piling up. Hunger sneaks in too, even if you fed them an hour ago. Sometimes, it's just their way of letting off steam. There isn't always a clear reason, but there are plenty of ways dads can get ahead of it.

The best defense is to anticipate the storm. Notice if your baby starts yawning, rubbing eyes, or gets extra clingy in the early evening. These are signs it's almost witching hour. If you can catch these cues early, sometimes a quick feed or nap can help head off a meltdown. Set the mood: lower the lights around the house, mute the TV, and keep stimulation to a minimum. Babies pick up on your energy. If you start moving slower and talking softer, they often follow suit.

When things kick off, you need a toolbox of soothing moves. Babywearing is my favorite. Strap your kid in a carrier and start pacing the living room or stroll outside if the weather permits. The rhythm of your walk plus your body heat often settles even the fussiest little one.

The "5 S's" from pediatrician Harvey Karp are legendary for a reason: shushing (loud enough to match their cries), swinging (gentle sways or bouncing on an exercise ball), sucking (pacifier or clean finger), side or stomach holding (only while you're watching them, never for sleep), and swaddling alternatives like sleep sacks if they're still under four months and not rolling. Though swaddling isn't the long-term answer, a snug sleep sack or your arms can create comfort without risk.

Turn on white noise; apps, fans, or dedicated machines all work. This background hum drowns out jarring household sounds and gives babies something steady to focus on. If you can't find a white noise machine fast enough, try running water in the bathroom or even softly humming yourself. Don't underestimate the "dad dance" either. A silly two-step in the kitchen or slow swaying with music can transform hysteria into giggles (or at least a quieter cry).

Keeping your sanity as a dad is just as important as soothing your baby. Tag-team with your partner: swap every twenty minutes so nobody feels like they're losing their mind. Prep easy dinners ahead, like frozen pizzas or slow cooker meals, so you don't add hunger to the stress mix.

Humor is a secret weapon; go ahead and narrate your baby's meltdown like a sports commentator or make faces until one of you cracks up. Playlists help too. Create one of calming music for your baby and one for yourself (sometimes punk rock is therapy). Podcasts are great for keeping your brain occupied while you rock endlessly.

Supporting your partner can turn a rough night into teamwork instead of tension. Don't try to fix everything; sometimes all they want is a nod and a "this sucks, but we've got this." A simple "want me to take over for a bit?" goes a long way. Knowing when to step in and when to offer space makes a huge difference.

Real stories make this real. I remember one dad who only survived those hours by doing laps around his kitchen with his son in a carrier while listening to jazz. He swears it was the trumpet solos that did the trick. Another friend tried every trick he could find online before realizing his daughter just wanted to be held skin-to-skin on his chest while he watched old baseball highlights. Sometimes what works one day flops the next; flexibility is key.

Here are some top dad-approved moves:

1. Walks outside with baby in a carrier

2. White noise on repeat

3. Low lights and soft talking

4. "Dad dance" routines with calming music

5. Calling in backup when patience runs out

There will be evenings when nothing seems to work. That doesn't mean you're failing; it just means your baby is being a baby. Some problems don't have instant fixes. Trust that being present and calm (or faking calm) actually does help your child, even if they're still crying.

To wrap up this chapter: every dad faces rough nights, but each one teaches you something new about your baby, and probably yourself. You'll build skills and patience you never knew you had, and even on the loudest nights, you're forging the bond that matters most. Next up, we'll dig into building connections with your little one every single month because it's not just about surviving, it's about growing together.

CHAPTER 3
Building Bonds: Dad and Baby Connection Month by Month

The Science and Art of Dad-Baby Bonding

Picture this: You're sitting on the couch, baby in your lap, both of you blinking under the glow of a late-night lamp. Maybe your newborn stares past your shoulder, maybe they yawn, or maybe they're just a warm little bundle snoozing on your chest. You might wonder, *"Is this what bonding is supposed to feel like?"*

Here's the thing: bonding doesn't always arrive with fireworks or movie-moment music. For some dads, it's instant. For others, it's slow, built through repetition, touch, and those quiet little moments when the world seems to pause and the only thing that matters is the person in your arms.

Let's break down what actually happens in your body and mind as you get to know your baby. Modern science confirms that you, as a dad, are not just a bystander to this experience. When you spend time holding, talking to, and caring for your baby, your brain chemistry shifts. Your body ramps up production of oxytocin, the so-called "love hormone." This isn't just a buzzword; oxytocin actually helps you feel calmer and more connected to your child. Prolactin, another hormone often linked with nurturing behavior, rises as well, especially after hands-on care or soothing routines. These changes aren't exclusive to moms; dads experience them too, especially with regular physical closeness and involvement.

It goes even deeper. Every time you hold your baby, make eye contact, or even just talk in that goofy "dad voice," you're sending signals that help wire their developing brain. Early touch, gentle pats, cuddles, or resting your baby against your chest—stimulates neural pathways crucial for emotional and sensory growth. Your voice becomes a familiar soundscape for your baby's world; studies show that hearing dad's voice regularly can help build language skills and emotional security. Presence isn't about doing everything perfectly; it's about showing up again and again, making your baby feel safe and known.

There's a myth out there that bonding is automatic, or that moms have some secret advantage dads can never match. It's just not true.

Sure, some parents feel an immediate connection, but many need more time. Maybe you're still waiting for that "aha" moment when the rush of love hits. Maybe you're worried because you haven't had one yet. That's normal. Research shows that many dads grow their bond through daily routines, bathing, diaper changes, reading stories, even if it starts out feeling awkward or forced. In fact, studies estimate upwards of 60% of dads describe their strongest connection forming during the everyday grind rather than magical first encounters.

The long-term benefits of early bonding show up in both you and your child. Kids with a strong attachment to their fathers tend to be more emotionally resilient. They bounce back from stress faster and show more curiosity about the world around them. These children usually develop richer vocabularies and better social skills by the time they reach school age. For dads, the payoff is real: those who bond early report less stress overall and greater confidence in their parenting abilities. Feeling connected also helps buffer against anxiety and makes it easier to ride out the tough nights or tantrum days.

If you're finding it tough to connect right now, you're not alone. I've talked to dads who said they felt more like a bodyguard than a parent at first, guarding naps, guarding peace and quiet, but not really feeling that spark. One dad told me it took three months before he felt anything beyond basic responsibility; another admitted he didn't feel "like a real dad" until his baby smiled at him for the first time.

There's no deadline for bonding; what matters is showing up and trying.

Reflection Exercise: Finding Your Bond

Grab a notebook or open your phone notes tonight after the baby goes down. Write out one thing, no matter how small, that made you feel close or at least present for your child today. Did you like the way their hand curled around your finger? Did they react to your goofy face or settle when you hummed a tune?

If nothing jumps out yet, jot down what you hope will help you connect: a walk together, reading aloud, or just narrating what you're doing as you hold them. Try this every few days. Looking back in a month or two, you'll see patterns form and probably notice moments of connection that felt invisible in real time.

Bonding isn't a contest or a test. It's a process made up of millions of tiny interactions stacked together over days and weeks. You're building something lasting each time you pause to listen, hold, or simply be there, even if you're also half-asleep or wondering what comes next. You've got more instincts than you think, and every day brings another chance to find your own way into this relationship.

Hands-On From Day One: Skin-to-Skin and Beyond

Picture yourself shirtless, your baby resting against your bare chest while you both breathe quietly. This is skin-to-skin contact. It's simple but deeply meaningful. Start by finding a private, warm spot, whether it's a hospital room, your bedroom, or a living room chair. Silence your phone, turn off distractions, and ensure the room is cozy for your undressed baby. Place your baby on your chest, cover you both with a blanket to retain warmth, and support their back and neck. Let your heartbeat soothe them. Skin-to-skin isn't limited to those first hours; it's equally valuable during hospital recovery, after baths, or during peaceful moments at home. Let your baby rest or move as long as you're both comfortable.

The golden hour after birth is ideal for skin-to-skin, but any time, hospital stay, at home, morning, or night, works. Those first days are hectic, but even ten minutes of this connection matters. If you missed skin-to-skin immediately post-birth, don't worry; it's never too late to start.

Physical bonding continues beyond the newborn phase. Babywearing is an excellent way to maintain closeness. Use a soft carrier or sling to keep your baby near as you go about your day, letting them enjoy your movement, scent, and voice. Walk around the block or gently move as you tidy up. Infant massage is another powerful bonding tool: gently massage their arms, legs, and back with baby-safe oil after a bath or before bed. This can calm fussy babies and strengthen your bond. Day-to-day playful touch, raspberries on tummies, lifting games, and gentle tickles also deepens your connection and makes routine moments special.

Feeling awkward is common. When I first tried skin-to-skin with my daughter, I felt exposed and uncertain, especially in the hospital.

My daughter squirmed; I doubted whether I was doing it "right." Other dads have similar worries, concerns about body hair, privacy, or feeling out of place. But after a few minutes, it often clicks: your baby's warmth calms you, and self-consciousness fades. If you feel nervous, try deep breathing or humming, focusing on the simple comfort between you and your child. There's no performance or right way, just real connection.

Many dads miss the immediate post-birth bonding window due to adoption, C-sections, NICU stays, or chaotic deliveries. Skin-to-skin is for every family, no matter the timing. Adoptive or non-birthing dads should start whenever possible, even weeks after birth. For NICU babies, kangaroo care (holding your diapered baby upright against your chest under a blanket) is incredibly valuable. Nurses can help arrange safe positions if your newborn has wires or monitors; don't hesitate to ask.

If you're anxious about looking awkward or making mistakes, realize every dad feels that way at first. Don't let nervousness stop you. Prepare your space in advance to avoid scrambling while holding your baby. If privacy is a concern, have your partner or nurse give you time alone. If your baby fusses initially, that's normal. Try again later, perhaps after a feed when they're calm.

Skin-to-skin adapts to all situations. If you can't be present (travel, deployment), have your partner use a blanket with your scent during baby cuddles. For adoption or surrogacy, begin skin-to-skin as soon as you're allowed. It immediately fosters attachment.

Interactive Exercise: Skin-To-Skin Confidence Builder

Set aside 10–20 minutes for skin-to-skin with your baby. Eliminate distractions, hold them close, and focus on their breathing and movements. After, jot down three words describing your feelings: awkward, peaceful, proud, sleepy, or anything else. Repeat weekly to see how your comfort and connection evolve.

Remember, skin-to-skin isn't about perfect technique. It's about being there, physically and emotionally, for your child, no matter how uncertain or clumsy it may feel at first.

Bonding Without Feeding: Creative Involvement for All Dads

Sometimes you end up feeling like a third wheel during feeding sessions, especially in those early months if your partner is breastfeeding or pumping. It's normal to wonder where you fit in when the spotlight keeps swinging away. But here's the secret: some of the strongest dad-baby bonds aren't built with a bottle or breast, but through the everyday routines you shape together. One of the simplest ways to carve out your own space is by taking charge of the morning routine. Start each day with a "dad greeting." Pick your own ritual, whether it's a silly song, a gentle stretch with your baby on your lap, or just opening the curtains and narrating what you see outside. Babies thrive on predictability, and your face, voice, and touch become anchor points in their day. If your child is already at the age where they're alert and responsive in the morning, make it your time for one-on-one giggles, mirror play, or even just a quiet cuddle while you sip your coffee. This becomes your thing, and it matters.

Bedtime is another golden opportunity. While feeding might be part of the pre-sleep routine, there's always room for a dad-only ritual. You can lead bath time and turn it into a comedy set: think rubber duck races and goofy bath time jokes, or claim storytime as your personal stage. Even if your baby can't follow the words yet, your voice and presence help them wind down. Make up a personalized lullaby (it doesn't have to rhyme), or pick a favorite book to read every night. Some dads invent bedtime "call-and-response" games. Maybe you say, "Goodnight toes!" and your baby wiggles their feet, or you count stuffed animals together before lights out. The trick is consistency; babies love knowing what comes next, and before long, these moments belong to both of you.

Want to be the king of tummy time? Set up play mat sessions with high-contrast toys or just stretch out next to your baby, talking about everything you see. Make silly faces, narrate your movements, or introduce simple games like "airplane arms" or tapping out rhythms on the mat. These sessions build strength for your baby and confidence for you. If you're feeling unsure what to say or do, just describe what's happening ("You're pushing up so strong!") or sing your favorite childhood song. If you're up for it, get down on their level and let them touch your beard, glasses, or fingers. Babies are fascinated by their dads' features.

Feeling left out during marathon nursing or pumping sessions happens to almost every dad. Instead of sitting in the background scrolling your phone, look for ways to redirect that energy into another connection point. Offer to burp the baby after feeds, change diapers right after, or plan a mini-adventure once feeding ends, maybe a lap around the house or stepping out on the porch for some fresh air together. If direct involvement feels impossible in those moments, prep something special for later, a playlist of calming tunes for bedtime, a silly hat for tomorrow's playtime, or even just laying out a fresh onesie with a note for your partner.

Scripts and rituals help make these routines stick. Try announcing bedtime with a "Dad's sleepy song" or inventing a morning cheer ("Rise and shine with Daddy time!"). Start bath time with a classic dad joke, corny puns are welcome here ("Why did the duck cross the tub? To get to the other tide!"). You might even invent your own gentle handshake or foot wiggle routine before putting on pajamas. The important thing is repetition; even if it feels goofy at first, your baby will start to anticipate these moments and respond in their own way.

To keep things fresh and challenge yourself as a new dad, give yourself mini-goals each week. Try the "one-on-one adventure" challenge: take your baby on a solo walk around the block (weather permitting), introduce them to new sounds in the backyard, or create an indoor scavenger hunt for soft toys. Another week, focus on low-key sensory games. Sit together in front of a mirror and mimic each other's faces, crinkle paper for sound exploration, or gently blow raspberries on their tummy to see if you can coax a giggle. Mark down any new reaction or skill you notice; these are signs your relationship is growing.

It's easy to get discouraged if you feel sidelined from feeding or if bonding doesn't happen overnight. The truth is that every dad has days when they feel like an extra in their own home movie. The key is persistence and creativity, finding rhythms that work for you and your child, even if they look nothing like what you imagined. Give yourself credit for showing up and experimenting; every routine you create becomes another thread in the fabric of your relationship with your child.

Dad-and-Baby Adventures: Month-by-Month Activity Guides

The first year with your baby is packed with newness. Every single month brings a different little person to your arms. Kicking things off in month one, you'll find your baby's world is small and their needs are simple. Gentle walks become golden. Wrap your baby snug in a carrier, step out into the air, and narrate the world as you stroll. Point out the neighbor's barking dog, the crunch of leaves, or the rhythm of rain on the sidewalk. Even if they sleep through it, the sound of your voice and the steady movement builds comfort.

Back at home, soft music, anything from jazz to lullabies, can fill the background as you rock together, creating a shared playlist of calm. Don't underestimate how even just lying together with your baby on your chest, breathing in sync, can be an adventure for both of you.

Three months in, your baby is getting more alert, and this is when play takes on a new meaning. Tummy time moves from being a battle to a game. Lay out a high-contrast mat or even a bold-patterned towel, and get down on their level. Make silly faces, mimic their little noises, wiggle a toy just out of reach. This is when you might see that first real grin just for you, a milestone all its own. Add in high-contrast toys, a black-and-white picture book, or even just a shiny kitchen spoon for entertainment. The goal isn't fancy gear but giving your baby's eyes and brain something to explore while you're right there cheering them on.

By six months, things ramp up again. It's peekaboo season. Babies start to understand object permanence, so covering your face with your hands and popping out with a goofy smile gets big laughs. Supported sitting opens up a new world: prop your baby with pillows and sit facing them, rolling a soft ball back and forth or clapping together to music. The weather's warming up? Take the stroller outside for longer rides. Narrate everything, talk about birds overhead, describe the smells of grass or a neighbor's barbecue drifting by. Even quick trips to the mailbox turn into an expedition if you keep up a running commentary.

At nine months, babies move fast. Crawling races across a rug or grass patch can turn a grumpy afternoon into giggles. Set up sensory bins, fill a shallow tub with safe objects like silicone spatulas, soft cloths, or textured toys, and let them explore as you talk about what they're touching. Crank up the music for "dad dance parties." Hold your baby tight or let them bop in your lap while you groove. They'll love the movement and your uninhibited silliness.

Twelve months brings new horizons. Your child is ready for their first playground adventure. Even if they're not walking solo yet, swings and slides (with your help) are pure joy. Try simple hide-and-seek behind trees or playground equipment; those peals of laughter will stick with you for years. Chase them around on all fours if they're crawling or tottering; they'll think you're hilarious.

Routine chores don't have to be boring for either of you. Turn grocery shopping into a scavenger hunt by pointing out colors, naming fruits, or letting them hold a (soft) item in the cart. Folding laundry? Narrate each step, "Here's Dad's blue sock! Where's yours?", and see if they'll help crumple shirts or toss socks into piles. These simple activities make everyday tasks feel like little games and strengthen your connection.

Dad adventures aren't just fun; they shape your baby's confidence and curiosity while giving you purpose beyond the daily grind. Each outing, no matter how small, helps them feel safe exploring the world with you nearby. You'll notice them scanning for your reaction when something new happens; they trust your cues on what's exciting or safe. As these routines become familiar, you'll see their eyes light up when you pull out their favorite book or get ready for another stroller ride.

Growth isn't just measured in inches or milestones; it lives in these moments when you both step outside your comfort zones together. Documenting these adventures adds another layer of meaning. Try jotting down monthly "dad win" journal entries, a quick note on what made you proud or laugh that month, even if it was just surviving a meltdown at Target without losing your marbles. Snap photos during outings or at home, messy breakfast faces, wild hair after bath time, that first trip down the slide, and turn them into a "first year with dad" photo collage for your wall or phone background.

Looking back at these memories, you'll realize how much you've both changed, and how many stories you've collected together along the way.

Handling Baby's Preference for the Other Parent

Many dads experience moments when their baby seems fixated on someone else, usually their partner. You might reach out, but your baby twists away or cries for mom. It stings and raises questions about your parenting, but this preference is normal and usually about familiarity, routine, and comfort. Babies bond most with the person who is around most often or provides primary care, especially between six and nine months, when separation anxiety develops and your baby learns you and your partner are truly separate people. While it feels personal, it's not a judgment on your abilities or love.

To stay connected, you need intention and creativity. Rather than withdrawing (even though it's tempting), create routines that build your relationship. Try getting up early for solo morning snuggles, even if it's only fifteen minutes of quiet rocking, or take over bath time once or twice a week and make it playful. When your partner is out, don't just see it as babysitting; take the opportunity to confidently engage: carry your baby while doing chores, narrate what you're doing, or sing a "dad song" that becomes your own ritual. Consistency is what matters. Even if your baby fusses for mom, persist with your routines. Over time, they'll become predictable and comforting.

Avoid letting resentment creep in by communicating openly with your partner. Establish and stick to routines so both of you know when you'll each have one-on-one time with your baby. If your child reaches for the other parent during a difficult moment, gently reassure your baby but don't immediately give in; finish the task and say, "Dad's here right now," with quiet confidence. This helps avoid undermining one another or competing for affection. Debrief together later about what's working or if anyone needs extra support.

Stories from other dads offer perspective during these phases. One father found himself always the "backup parent," and every attempt to soothe his son was met with crying for mom. However, he kept going: daily walks, goofy bath routines, a unique dad peekaboo voice. One day, with mom gone and his son upset after a nap, he picked him up expecting resistance, but the boy calmed down and cuddled in. That was the turning point, and after that, bedtime stories became their thing. Another dad shared that his daughter preferred mom for months, until a weekend road trip forced six hours of solo time together. After that, she reached happily for him at home, showing how patience and consistent presence pay off.

These phases can shift without warning. One week you're ignored; the next, you're the hero who gets the giggle or calms teething tears. Babies don't tally the days; they remember the presence and persistence. When frustration builds (and it will), remember this doesn't last forever. Your consistent effort forms the bonds your child will rely on as they grow.

Staying involved means showing up even when it's tough. Don't wait for an invitation; carve out solo moments and treat them as opportunities, not pass-fail tests. Sometimes connection builds during unexpected times, a giggle at a chaotic diaper change or a quiet moment during a walk. These memories create trust and comfort that outlast any phase or temporary preference.

Working as a team with your partner strengthens your family and benefits your child. When both parents stick to routines and support each other in front of the baby, you send the message that both of you are safe and reliable. If you haven't had that moment of being chosen yet, keep showing up. Eventually, those little arms will reach for you, and when that happens, all your patience will be worth it.

Spotlight Stories: Connection Wins from Diverse Dads

Real connection with your child doesn't come with instructions, and every dad finds his own way. From talking with other dads, it's obvious there are countless ways to build meaningful bonds, no matter your background or family setup. Take Marcus, a single dad who adopted his son after years of waiting. On adoption day, he began drawing tiny smiley faces on his son's toes, a simple ritual that became their cherished "thing." Each morning, despite any chaos, Marcus would doodle a face, inventing funny stories about those toes. It created a lighthearted moment for both and gave his son something to look forward to each day.

Owen co-parents with his husband, and their daughter joined them after a tough NICU stay. Feeling overwhelmed and out of place, Owen started "Superhero Story Hour." Instead of just reading, he invented tales where their daughter was the hero, building rockets from pillows or outsmarting dragons. This ritual made bedtime fun, helped them bond as a family, and created a sense of team spirit. James, another dad, lives with a physical disability, making some activities difficult. Rather than focus on what he couldn't do, he embraced his strengths, like voice acting. Every bath became a "radio show," with James voicing pirates or undersea adventurers. Bath time became a highlight, showing that connection comes from energy and intention, not just physical activity.

These rituals don't have to be elaborate. A dad started a "Daddy-Daughter Breakfast Club" at the local diner every Saturday, just him, his toddler, and animal-shaped pancakes. That simple routine became their special time to bond. Another friend snapped a selfie before every morning walk with his son, creating a growing timeline of their relationship. Secret handshakes, silly dances during commercials, or a special shoulder tap before bed: all these routines become anchors in a child's memory. It doesn't matter if you parent solo, with a partner, or in a blended family; traditions are yours to create.

What stands out is that creativity matters more than perfection. Keep experimenting until you find your "signature move," the thing your kid will remember as uniquely "dad." Maybe it's a made-up diaper-changing song, a dance before nap, or something else entirely. The first attempt may be awkward, but kids love repetition and will show you what they enjoy.

If you're not sure where to begin, pick a routine part of the day, like getting dressed or cleaning up, and make it playful. Narrate it like a sports game, or challenge your child to a funny face contest. As you get more comfortable and your child engages, these small moments can become the best part of your day.

If you worry your bond isn't strong because of work, shared custody, or nerves, let these stories reassure you. Every dad brings something unique. All kids need are small, consistent signals that say, "I want to spend time with you." Whether it's ten minutes at bedtime or an hour on weekends, the more you show up, the stronger your connection will be.

Celebrate Your Win

Pause tonight and notice a moment that went right, a smile at storytime, a giggle at breakfast, a hug as you buckle your child in. Mark it in your mind or jot it down. It doesn't have to be big, just real and yours. If you like, start a "connection wins" list: each week, record one moment when you felt truly present with your child. Over time, you'll see just how many wins you have.

There is no single way to be "the connected dad." It's about being open, trying, and showing up in ways that feel right for your family. Whether it's superhero tales or weekend pancakes, your presence is what counts.

Connection isn't built on grand gestures; it's found in small rituals, silly smiles, and daily habits you make your own. As we finish this chapter on building bonds, remember: little moments matter most. Next, we'll dig into supporting your partner, because being a great dad also means being there for the whole family.

CHAPTER 4
Supporting Your Partner: Postpartum, Teamwork, and Real Talk

Recognizing and Responding to Postpartum Mood Changes

Bringing home your baby might feel like entering a new world. One full of exhaustion and chaos, but also unpredictable mood swings. You may find yourself unsure how to respond as your partner's emotions shift dramatically from laughter to tears. One friend likened it to a house of mirrors, never quite knowing who you'll encounter next. This invisible, emotional rollercoaster is a typical part of the early postpartum period. While sometimes it's just temporary "baby blues," other times it's more serious. Your support as a new dad truly matters.

Almost all new moms experience postpartum blues, a wave of mood swings, irritability, anxiety, sadness, and crying that appears within days of birth and may last a few weeks. These mood changes come without much warning. Your partner may shift from lovingly watching over your baby to being upset about something minor. This is normal: her body is recovering, and hormones are fluctuating wildly. Usually, baby blues don't get in the way of her caring for your baby or you, and there are still moments of brightness.

However, sometimes these feelings don't subside, becoming more persistent and disruptive; this is postpartum depression (PPD). Unlike the blues, PPD stays for weeks or even months and can involve a range of symptoms. Your partner might start withdrawing from you or the baby, passing off care tasks, or avoiding affection and citing the need for space. You might notice ongoing, intense crying, uncharacteristic anger, or restlessness that doesn't ease with sleep.

Other signs include insomnia even when the baby sleeps, spacing out during conversation, loss of appetite, binge eating, headaches, or panic attacks. Listen carefully if she voices doubts about being a good mom or expresses hopelessness. There's also postpartum anxiety, racing thoughts, and constant worry that something may happen to the baby. Very rarely, postpartum psychosis can occur, including confusion or hallucinations—a medical emergency that requires immediate attention.

What can you do? Trust your instincts; you know your partner best. If you sense something is wrong, don't wait. Approach with empathy, not judgment. Avoid dismissive advice like "Just get some sleep." Instead, try: "I've noticed you seem down this week, do you want to talk?" or "It looks like you're having a tough time lately; I'm here for you." You don't have to solve the problem, just let her know she's not alone. If she's not ready to talk, just being there speaks volumes.

Active listening is crucial now. Eliminate distractions and give her your full attention. Use reflective listening: "So you're feeling overwhelmed every night when it gets dark?" Unless she asks, don't offer fixes. Just listening can ease her burden.

If symptoms persist over two weeks or intensify, seek outside help. It might feel uncomfortable to suggest therapy or professional support, but frame it gently: "I care about you and want us to be strong for our baby. I think talking to someone could help." Offer to help find a therapist or be there for the first call or appointment. If therapy feels too daunting, suggest talking with a trusted friend or family member. Build a ready list of resources such as postpartum support groups, mental health hotlines, or online communities.

Interactive Element: Quick Mood Change Checklist for Dads

- Has my partner withdrawn from me or our baby?

- Is she crying excessively or showing unexplained anger?

- Is she unable to sleep, even when exhausted?

- Any sudden appetite changes?

- Is she feeling hopeless or like a "bad mom"?

- Signs of panic attacks: racing heart, dizziness, shaking?

- Any mention of seeing or hearing things that aren't real?

Check more than two boxes (especially if symptoms last more than two weeks)? Reach out for professional support.

Supporting your partner during postpartum mood swings isn't about fixing everything; it's about being present, listening, and knowing when to get help so your family can move forward.

The Partner Support Playbook: Small Actions, Big Impact

There's no medal for "Most Helpful Dad," but if there were, it would go to the guy who steps in before anyone asks. The biggest difference you can make isn't about grand gestures; it's the little things done every day. You start by scanning the room: dishes piling up, laundry basket overflowing, trash can threatening to erupt. Instead of waiting for a nudge, you roll up your sleeves and get to work.

Taking on chores without being asked isn't about earning points; it's about showing that you're in this together. You empty the dishwasher while your partner feeds the baby. You wipe down counters and prep the next round of bottles while she catches her breath. On days when she's glued to the couch feeding or pumping, a glass of water and a snack tray within reach is a lifeline. It's these unsung acts, refilling her water before she asks, making sure there's fresh fruit or a granola bar nearby, that say "I see you, I've got you."

Managing visitors is its own level of support. Friends and family mean well, but their timing can be less than ideal. You become the gatekeeper, texting back, "Now's not great, but we'll let you know when we're ready for company." Sometimes you have to be direct, setting boundaries so your partner isn't stuck making small talk when she'd rather nap or just exist in stretchy pants. Protecting her space is an invisible shield she'll never forget.

Anticipating needs is almost like learning a new language; one spoken with raised eyebrows, weary sighs, or silence. Maybe you notice she's gone quiet or her eyelids droop in the afternoon light. Instead of asking, "Do you want to rest?" you scoop up the baby and say, "I'm heading out for a walk, take a nap." You run the bathwater without waiting for a request, light a candle, and usher her in for twenty minutes of quiet while you handle the chaos outside the door. Sometimes it's as simple as taking over baby duty so she can eat with both hands or shower without the soundtrack of newborn cries.

Invisible labor is everywhere, lists in your partner's head you probably never see. She tracks feeding schedules, doctor appointments, when to order more diapers, and if there's enough formula on hand for tomorrow. You step up by grabbing your phone and setting reminders for pediatrician visits or updating the shared calendar with vaccine appointments. You keep an eye on baby supplies and reorder before things run low. If your fridge looks sad or the pantry shelf is bare, you build a quick grocery list and hit the store, or order delivery if that's all you've got in you. Organizing meals takes stress off her plate; maybe you set up a meal train with friends or batch-cook simple dinners to stash in the freezer.

Real-life stories drive this home. One mom told me her husband left a sticky note on the bathroom mirror every Monday: "You're tougher than you think." Another dad ran out to buy her favorite ice cream at 10 p.m., no special reason other than he remembered she'd mentioned craving it days ago. A friend described how her partner started keeping a shared to-do list on their phones; whenever he finished something (restocked wipes, paid a bill), he marked it off without being prompted. It sounds small, but seeing those tasks disappear made her feel less alone.

Encouragement often comes in quiet moments, like slipping an "I love you" note into her robe pocket or texting a silly meme when she's stuck under a sleeping baby. Sometimes it's running interference with that one well-meaning aunt who always overstays ("We're heading to nap time now, let's catch up another day"). Other times it's about action, like taking over nighttime rocking so your partner can get two uninterrupted hours of sleep.

A shared to-do list, physical or digital, becomes your playbook. You update it without needing reminders, so she doesn't have to carry every detail in her head. Maybe you make it a habit to check that list every morning; if you see "call pediatrician" or "order more burp cloths," you just do it. These things don't go unnoticed; they add up.

What matters most isn't perfection; it's effort that says "I'm here," "I care," and "We're doing this together." The little actions, the ones that might seem invisible, are often the ones that stick for years to come. Take pride in noticing what needs to be done without being told and acting before exhaustion sets in. That kind of support shifts everything, not just for your partner, but for your whole family.

Communication Scripts for Tough Conversations

Nobody tells you how awkward it can get trying to talk about the tough stuff when you're both running on caffeine, nerves, and barely three hours of sleep. You want to keep things calm, but sometimes it feels like any topic, who does more diapers, why nobody's in the mood for sex, or even who forgot to buy wipes, can turn into a standoff. Most couples hit this wall, and it's not a sign you're failing; it's just real life with a new baby.

What helps is having a few ready-to-go scripts for opening hard conversations without starting a fight. Start simple and keep your tone curious, not accusatory. Try: "I've noticed you seem distant lately. Can we talk about it?" or "I feel like we're both on edge. Is there something I'm missing?" For resentment, use gentle honesty: "It feels like I'm dropping the ball lately. How are you holding up?"

If the intimacy topic feels radioactive, approach it with vulnerability: "I miss being close. Can we figure out how to reconnect, even if it's just in small ways right now?" And for disagreements about parenting style, such as routine versus flexibility, screen time, or sleep training, open with, "I see things a little differently. Can we talk through what matters most to us?"

Active listening isn't rocket science, but it does take effort, especially when your brain is scattered and you're itching to jump in with a fix. The key is slowing down and echoing back what you hear: "What I'm hearing is that you feel overwhelmed and need help with bath time," or "So you're saying it stings when I correct you in front of your parents."

Use your body language to show you're present: put your phone down, make eye contact, nod occasionally, and resist the urge to cross your arms or roll your eyes. If you feel yourself clenching your jaw or staring out the window, reset by leaning forward a bit or mirroring your partner's posture. Sometimes physical cues speak louder than words.

When things start getting heated, it's easy to slip into fight-or-flight mode, voices rise, sarcasm creeps in, or someone storms off. Rather than letting arguments spiral, agree ahead of time on a "pause" word or gesture, a neutral phrase like "timeout," or even something silly like "banana," that signals you both need a break before saying something regrettable. If either of you calls for a pause, honor it without rolling your eyes or muttering under your breath. Step away for five minutes, splash cold water on your face, and come back when you're both less likely to escalate.

Checking in before tempers flare can save hours of silent treatment later. Schedule a weekly "relationship huddle." It sounds cheesy, but it works wonders. Choose a low-stress time (maybe after baby goes down for the night), grab snacks or tea, and ask each other three questions: *What went well this week? What was tough? How can I support you better next week?*

Use this space to hash out recurring issues, who gets up for the 4 a.m. feed, or how to handle grandparent visits, before resentment festers. My partner and I called this our "State of the Union," and some weeks we only lasted ten minutes before passing out, but even that short check-in kept us from bottling up annoyances.

Journaling before a hard talk helps clarify what's really bugging you. Jot down what you want to say and why it matters. Sometimes, writing out your thoughts cools the emotional charge before you open your mouth. Try prompts like: *What's really bothering me? What do I hope will change? Is there something I haven't said out loud yet?* You might realize you're not actually mad about dishes but feeling invisible after a rough week.

If you reach an impasse, say, nobody wants to be "the default parent" at night, try brainstorming together for creative fixes instead of sticking to old patterns. Maybe you alternate nights on duty, or use a coin toss for those extra-tough mornings. One dad shared how he and his wife used a shared calendar to plot out who handled which nights; another couple traded off early mornings versus late bedtimes based on work schedules.

The point isn't always perfect harmony. Sometimes, just knowing you can talk honestly without someone blowing up is enough. These scripts and routines turn conflict into connection, or at least keep things from boiling over. Real communication gets messy sometimes, but with practice and patience, it gets easier, and might even bring a few laughs at how hard both of you are trying.

Nighttime Feedings: How to Truly Share the Load

The reality of parenthood hits hardest during middle-of-the-night feedings. At 2 a.m., "sharing the load" isn't just a nice phrase; it's crucial to survival and sanity. When you wake up to a crying baby and lock eyes with your equally exhausted partner, know that this is the essence of early family life. There's no universal fix, but there are ways to make nights less stressful, more balanced, and a little less isolating.

Start by tailoring your approach to your family's feeding style. With bottle-fed babies, equality is possible: alternate nights or split the night into shifts (e.g., 7 p.m.–1 a.m. and 1 a.m.–7 a.m.), giving both parents a solid stretch of sleep. For breastfeeding families, teamwork has a different look. While only one parent can nurse, preparing bottles, water, and snacks before bed helps. Keep clean bottles and parts within arm's reach, prep a water bottle and snacks, and set up everything you'll need nearby. Partners can handle diaper changes and burping, allowing the nursing parent to focus only on feeding, then helping soothe the baby back to sleep.

Small gestures matter, especially if your partner is breastfeeding. Those moments when you might want to drift back to sleep, instead offer company, a back rub, water, or a quick snack. Even just sitting together can be a comfort and a reminder that you're in this together.

Fatigue often leads to resentment if left unchecked. The old "sleep when the baby sleeps" advice applies to both parents. Take turns napping and be fair with sleeping in after tough nights. Some couples set clear policies: if you're up for the first shift, go to bed after dinner while your partner handles bedtime routines, then switch for the next night or shift. Try trading mornings, too: one gets up early with the baby, the other sleeps in.

A bit of creativity goes a long way. Some couples keep a whiteboard in the kitchen to track shifts. A visual log helps clear up confusion and keeps things light in the haze of sleep deprivation. Others listen to audiobooks or podcasts during feeds, turning those early hours into a mini date. Sharing your "night shift playlist" or chatting about a book in the morning gives you something to look forward to and share.

Families with older kids might create visual schedules or magnet boards so everyone knows who's on duty, no confusion, no excuses.

Working parents sometimes prep bottles before their shift, so their partner can grab and go with minimum fuss.

With combo feeding, you have more flexibility. Pumped milk or formula opens up the option for one parent to handle full overnight feeds while the other rests. Decide on a plan, alternate full nights off, or take turns every other night. Using formula or pumped milk so everyone gets rest is perfectly valid if it protects your family's well-being.

Small tweaks can make a big difference. Keeping a cooler with prepped bottles by your bed, or a stash of diapers, wipes, and pacifiers within reach, reduces nighttime scrambling. These adjustments can turn a chaotic night into a manageable one.

The emotional component shouldn't be overlooked. Sharing a joke, a glance, or a silly ritual can transform exhausting feeds into moments of connection. Some couples enjoy a nightly playlist or a goodnight phrase to bring routine and some lightness to sleep-deprived nights.

Open communication is key. If one partner feels overwhelmed or stuck with more than their share, talk about it and adjust your strategy together. Needs shift as babies grow, so stay flexible and regularly check in with each other to keep things fair.

Ultimately, no one gets enough sleep during these early months, but sharing night feeds is about more than rest; it's about ongoing commitment to each other. And sometimes, it's about finding a way to laugh together at 4 a.m., listening to an audiobook about Viking history, rocking your baby back to sleep, knowing you're not alone.

Navigating Physical Recovery: What Dads Need to Know

Watching your partner recover after childbirth is often a surprising challenge for new dads. Birth is hard on the body, whether it's a vaginal delivery, C-section, or a complicated experience. Recovery varies for everyone, but there are some constants.

Bleeding after birth is normal; think of a heavy period lasting a few weeks, meaning pads everywhere and absolutely no tampons. Pain is common too, sometimes sharp or just a dull ache. Vaginal births may involve swelling, stitches, or tearing, making sitting and moving uncomfortable. C-sections bring their own challenges: a surgical wound, strict lifting limits, and infection risk. Recovery timelines are personal. Some moms are up in a few days, others need weeks, but most take at least six weeks (sometimes more) to start feeling normal.

Mobility is usually difficult at first. Just getting out of bed or walking a short distance can hurt. For C-sections, your partner shouldn't lift anything heavier than the baby; the incision needs time to heal. That means you handle laundry baskets, older kids, the vacuum, and heavy lifting.

Watch for infection warning signs: redness, swelling, oozing, or fever, and call the doctor if you notice any. After a vaginal birth, keep an eye out for clots larger than a golf ball, foul-smelling discharge, or escalating pain. Any of these are reasons to call her OB or midwife.

Your main role right now is comfort. Help with whatever makes life easier. If standing or reaching hurts her, fetch the baby, carry the car seat, and push the stroller. Take care of pets or older kids so she can rest. Encourage her to sit and rest; you might need to insist. Jump in on practical tasks and let her know it's okay to take it easy.

What to avoid? Don't push her to "bounce back." Recovery is not a competition. Never question how long she's sore or suggest she should just "walk it off." Instead, set up comfortable spots for her to nurse or cuddle the baby, offer help with showers or dressing if needed, but back off if she wants space.

You can make a big difference through tangible tasks: Take over laundry, babies make a mountain of dirty clothes. Handle the washing, folding, and putting away so she doesn't have to ask. Take over kitchen duty: cook, clean, order in, and keep snacks handy. Take care of as many diaper changes as you can; it's more help than you'd think, sparing her extra bending and lifting. Keep the house tidy; even simple cleaning makes the home feel less chaotic, giving her one less thing to worry about.

Being an advocate is key. Relatives and friends may want to visit before your partner is ready. Be her gatekeeper: handle calls and texts, firmly say visits can wait, and don't let anyone pressure her to play host. At postpartum checkups, bring up questions: How's her bleeding? Is healing on track? What's normal pain? Anything to watch for? Speak up if you need more info. Appointments can be rushed, and it's easy for concerns to get overlooked.

After my partner's C-section, I quickly realized how much more support she needed. She couldn't twist at all for the first week, so I handled diaper changes, stairs, and night rocking. We made a recovery nest in the living room so she could rest without moving much. I also learned how essential it was to set boundaries with family. Sometimes the best thing you can do is insist she rest, not entertain.

Recovery is often unpredictable, with good days and setbacks. But showing up, asking questions, running interference with visitors, and managing household duties gives your partner the space she needs to heal. That builds trust and shows you're truly in it together for every up and down ahead.

Team No Sleep: Surviving Together and Avoiding Resentment

Sleep deprivation is like a fog that settles in every corner of your house. It doesn't just steal your energy, it plays tricks on your mind, colors your mood, and tests your relationship in ways you never saw coming. You find yourself reaching for patience that just isn't there. Suddenly, small annoyances feel huge. You'll wonder why you're snapping at the person you love or why you both keep forgetting what you walked into the kitchen for.

Mood swings become routine, and frustration can rise out of nowhere. You may catch yourself feeling on edge, irritable, even a bit resentful about whose turn it is to change a diaper or who last woke up with the baby. This isn't a sign that something is wrong with you or your relationship; it's a completely normal response to chronic exhaustion. Your brain and body are simply stretched to their limit.

When everything feels overwhelming, survival mode kicks in. Instead of trying to do it all, it's time to divide and conquer. Honestly, this is the secret sauce for making it through those early months as a team. Sit down together and figure out who does what, even if you need to renegotiate every day. If one of you handles the morning shift, the other gets the next nap window, even if it's only twenty minutes stolen behind a closed door.

Scheduling mini-breaks isn't selfish; it's how you keep each other going. Maybe you agree that when one parent taps out, the other steps in without rolling their eyes or keeping score. A shared running joke can help. A silly code word for when exhaustion hits max level lets you both signal, "Hey, I'm about to lose it," without sparking a fight. My partner and I used "zombie mode" as our cue; one mention and we knew it was time for backup or a five-minute solo break. These tiny agreements build trust and buffer against resentment.

No matter how much you love each other, tired brains lead to sharp words. You might get snappy about nothing or bicker over whose turn it is to clean bottles, only to regret it an hour later. Learning how to apologize quickly is a huge relief for both of you. It's as simple as saying, "Sorry for snapping at you, I'm just exhausted." The key is not making excuses or dragging out the moment. Accept that tired arguments happen and let forgiveness flow faster than blame. Resetting after a rough patch means letting things go, don't rehash every squabble or keep a mental tally of mistakes. Sometimes, a quick hug or a shared laugh after an argument is all it takes to get back on the same side.

Small wins deserve big celebrations, especially on the nights when everything feels like chaos. Maybe your baby finally slept for three hours straight, or one of you managed to make coffee without waking the whole house. These victories may seem trivial from the outside, but inside your home, they're worth gold. One night, my partner and I hit our breaking point and just started dancing in the living room at 3 a.m., baby in arms, music on low, laughing so we wouldn't cry. That moment stuck with us as a reminder that sometimes silliness is survival.

Keeping a sense of humor helps soften the hardest nights. Share those "parent wins" out loud: "We both survived until sunrise!" or "Nobody cried during bath time!" If words aren't your thing, try jotting down small wins on sticky notes and plastering them somewhere visible: a fridge, bathroom mirror, or even the coffee maker. Over time, those colorful scraps become a wall of proof that you've weathered storms together and found joy in the mess.

A shared gratitude journal can work wonders too. Each night, write down one thing, no matter how small, that went right or made you smile. Maybe it's as simple as, "Thankful for five minutes of quiet," or "Loved your pancakes this morning." This tiny ritual shifts your focus from what's going wrong to what you're building together.

In the end, team no sleep isn't about thriving; it's about sticking together when things are tough and refusing to let exhaustion pull you apart. You'll look back on these nights someday with more pride than regret, not because they were easy, but because you got through them side by side.

Sleep deprivation will challenge your patience, humor, and bond with your partner, but facing it as a team makes all the difference. Stay united through exhaustion and arguments by leaning on each other and celebrating every win, no matter how small. Up next: we'll talk about balancing life outside the home, work, finances, and finding time for yourself, because keeping your family strong means taking care of every part of your life.

CHAPTER 5
Dad Health: Mental, Emotional, and Physical Well-being

Dad Stress Is Real: Recognizing the Signs

Picture yourself pacing the hallway at 4 a.m., cradling a fussy baby while your coffee sits untouched. You're exhausted, unsure if you're asleep or awake, and the pressure to be the steadfast dad can feel overwhelming. This is the unfiltered side of fatherhood few discuss, the kind of stress that's more than just lost sleep. Most new dads expect to be tired, but stress appears in far more forms than most realize.

It's one thing to feel tired; it's another to be so drained you forget what day it is. New dad stress often outlasts a good nap. You might feel a heavy weight that doesn't lift even after rest, or find yourself more irritable, snapping at small annoyances, like toys clattering or persistent phone alerts. Sometimes, you might instead feel numb and disconnected, almost like you're watching life happen from underwater. This isn't weakness; it's your mind dealing with overwhelm.

Physical symptoms of stress can be subtle. Maybe you're nursing daily headaches, digestive issues, tight shoulders, stubborn heartburn, or persistent muscle tension. If you find yourself reaching for painkillers or massaging your temples more than usual, your body is signaling that things aren't right.

Stress often builds slowly and subtly. You might pull away without noticing, spending time scrolling on your phone in another room rather than interacting with your partner or baby. Escapist habits like binge-watching, late-night snacking, or gaming can creep in, not from hunger or interest, but to avoid what's weighing on you. Trouble focusing is another sign: maybe you reread emails or forget simple tasks. If you find yourself zoning out or feeling like nothing "sticks," pay attention; these are classic stress signals.

What makes this tricky is that withdrawing or seeking distractions can seem harmless. Everyone needs downtime, but when withdrawal or constant tech use becomes your norm, it's a warning sign. Some dads mistake this for a "normal adjustment," but avoiding connection is different than recharging with some alone time.

It's hard to discern when everyday stress tips into something deeper, like depression, anxiety, or burnout. The line gets crossed when, for more than two weeks, you've lost interest in things you love, feel overwhelmed daily, or every day feels too much to handle. That's more than stress. Anxiety may hit as constant worry or restless energy, while burnout feels like unshakable exhaustion, no matter how much you sleep.

When to Worry: Quick Self-Check

- You feel hopeless or empty most days.

- You lose interest in old hobbies or what brings you joy.

- Sleep issues go beyond interrupted nights, insomnia, or wanting to sleep all the time.

- Small problems cause you to feel overwhelmed fast.

- It's tough to connect with your partner or baby for several days.

- Your appetite changes a lot (eating much more or less).

- You fantasize about escaping, not just for a short break, but disappearing.

If several of these signs are familiar and don't improve with time or simple support, consider reaching out for help.

You don't have to face this alone. Self-reflection isn't about blaming yourself; it's about noticing changes before they spiral. Try a weekly check-in with yourself: "What's different since the baby?" "Am I avoiding my family or favorite things?" "Is stress showing as anger or numbness?" If something feels off, that's important.

Many dads miss the signs: one dad took every night feed and extra work shift until his body gave out; another wrote off tension and mood swings as "normal tiredness," only to realize months later he hadn't really laughed in weeks. These aren't rare cases; they show that stress isn't always obvious.

Talking openly about stress matters. You wouldn't ignore your car's warning lights; don't ignore your own. Regularly checking in and being honest is the first step to feeling better and to being present for your family as your true self.

Five-Minute Reset: Micro Self-Care for Sleep-Deprived Dads

If you ever wondered who invented the phrase "running on fumes," it was probably a new dad. Between night feedings, endless laundry, and the day job that expects you to pretend you slept, your mind and body get stretched thin. The idea of "self-care" might make you roll your eyes. Who has time for bubble baths or long gym sessions? The good news is, you don't need hours or a Zen retreat to feel better. Micro self-care is about squeezing tiny, meaningful resets into the cracks of your day; five minutes here and there can have a bigger impact than you'd expect.

One of my go-to moves is box breathing. It's dead simple: breathe in for four seconds, hold for four, out for four, hold again for four. Repeat a few times. Try it in the car before walking back into the house, or while waiting for the bottle to warm up. If that feels too structured, the "4-7-8 method" is another option: inhale for four seconds, hold for seven, exhale for eight. This longer exhale helps your heart rate slow and signals your body to chill out, even when your brain's buzzing with a dozen worries at once. You don't need a mat, candles, or an app, just air and attention.

When you feel trapped indoors and your legs haven't moved except between the couch and the crib, step outside for a five-minute walk. Even just circling the block resets your headspace. Fresh air clears cobwebs and changes your perspective. If you can't leave the house, stretch it out: reach up, touch your toes, roll your shoulders. It's less about flexibility and more about breaking the "couch potato" spell that creeps in after hours of sitting or pacing with a baby in your arms.

For those times when escape seems impossible, even the bathroom can be your sanctuary. I call it "bathroom break meditation." Lock the door, close your eyes, and just notice the feeling of sitting still. Nobody's asking you for anything. You get one minute just to hear yourself breathe. Don't feel guilty, everyone needs a moment to hit pause, even if it's behind a closed door.

Music changes everything. Pop in headphones for a favorite song; even half a song can jolt your mood out of a spiral. Or fire up a short podcast segment; five minutes of laughter or a voice you enjoy helps you reset. If you're feeding the baby solo, let a playlist run in the background while you rock. Suddenly, even the most repetitive routine feels less isolating.

Some days, creativity is required to snag rest. Power naps in the car, those 10 minutes reclined in the driveway, sometimes feel like winning the lottery. If naps aren't possible, try a two-minute gratitude journal in your notes app or on a sticky note. Write three things that didn't suck today: "baby smiled at me," "coffee was hot," "partner laughed at my joke." Small moments matter more than big ones when you're running low.

You don't need elaborate prep or fancy equipment for these resets. Dad hacks are all about making use of what's at hand. Stash a snack in the glove box for late-night drives back from the store. Keep a reusable water bottle nearby. You'll be shocked at how often dehydration feels like exhaustion or crankiness. If your partner is around, tag them in and step outside for a deep breath or two under the sky.

These micro-breaks aren't selfish; they're fuel for better parenting. Taking five minutes for yourself can flip your mood from "I can't deal" to "I've got this." You'll catch yourself snapping less, listening with more patience, and actually enjoying the little moments rather than wishing them away. I remember one meltdown evening where I almost lost my temper over spilled milk (literally). I put my son down safely in his crib, stepped outside for five long breaths, and came back with enough calm to clean up and laugh about it later.

Mood Shift Visual: Before and After Micro-Break

Draw a quick chart in your journal with two columns: "Before Break" and "After Break." Rate your mood from 1 (frazzled) to 10 (chill). Notice how even a five-minute reset can bump you up a notch or two on that scale.

Don't underestimate these tiny routines. When used regularly, they stack up to real change: your patience grows, frustration fades faster, and you recover from setbacks with more ease. It's not about being perfect; it's about giving yourself permission to pause before you reach your breaking point. Small resets teach your brain, and your family, that dads deserve care too.

When to Ask for Help: A No-Shame FAQ

Admitting you're struggling, especially as a new dad, can be tough. There's an old myth that you should handle everything alone, tough it out, and never let anyone see you struggle. Maybe you've told yourself, "Just man up," or "It's just tiredness." But thinking like that keeps many dads from getting the help they need. Pride, fear of judgment, or not wanting to look weak builds walls between you and support that could make things better. Many dads wait months before reaching out, thinking asking for help means failure, but it actually means you care enough to want things to improve.

Wondering if your feelings are "normal" is common. Everyone feels off sometimes, but if you're stuck, constant irritability, sadness, or feeling disconnected from your family, it's worth talking about. Maybe you aren't sleeping, you're snapping at everyone, or you keep thinking your family would be better off without you. If these feelings last more than a couple of weeks, don't ignore them. Reaching out sooner can help things get better faster.

Starting the conversation doesn't have to be complicated. If talking to your partner feels awkward, try saying: "I haven't been feeling like myself," or "I think I need to talk to someone, even if I'm not sure what's wrong." You don't need to have it all figured out, just open the door. With friends, honesty is key. Say, "Hey, have you ever felt like you can't get out of a funk?" or "I could use some backup right now." You might find they've felt the same and are ready to listen. If you'd rather not talk face-to-face, a text or a meme can also help break the ice.

Talking to a doctor might seem intimidating, but you won't be the first new parent they've seen. Simply say, "I'm having trouble coping since the baby arrived. I feel anxious, sad, or angry all the time." They'll guide you from there and suggest resources that suit you. If you're concerned you'll forget details, jot down a few notes before your appointment: main symptoms, when they started, and what makes them better or worse.

Here's a quick FAQ for dads:

- **"Is it normal to feel this bad?"**

Short-term stress is expected; if misery or hopelessness lingers, it's time to reach out.

- **"Will people think less of me if I ask for help?"**
No. Most people respect honesty and courage. Asking for help is about caring for your family, not your ego.
- **"What if I don't know what to say?"**
Start with "I'm not okay," or "I need some support." That's enough.
- **"Who do I call?"**

If things are urgent, like thoughts of self-harm, call a helpline right away. For ongoing stress, reach out to your doctor or a therapist.

Quick Resource List for Dads Ready to Reach Out

- **National hotlines:** Call the National Suicide Prevention Lifeline (1-800-273-8255) 24/7.

- **Dad-specific support:** Postpartum Support International offers a dad helpline and online chat.

- **Apps:** Try Headspace for mindfulness or Moodfit for mood tracking.

- **Local groups:** Search Facebook or Meetup for local or virtual new dad groups.

- **Therapists:** Use Psychology Today to find local therapists, including those specializing in men's and fathers' mental health.

Other dads confirm: asking for help changes things. One dad wrote, "The first call was the hardest, but all I got was understanding." Another said, "My partner just wanted honesty. When I opened up, we both cried, but we started solving things together."

A favorite quote from a dad: "I thought real strength was never needing help. Turns out, real strength is asking for it anyway." There's no reward for suffering in silence. Sometimes the bravest thing is admitting you're not okay and taking the first step toward feeling better. Your family needs you healthy and happy, not just toughing it out every day.

Managing Anxiety About "Doing It Right"

If you've ever sat holding your squirming baby, heart pounding with worries of "Am I messing this up?" you're not alone. Nearly every dad feels some level of anxiety about being "good enough." Nobody warns you that self-doubt comes standard with parenthood. There's constant pressure to get it all right: bottle temps, sleep schedules, diaper changes, partner support, and work responsibilities. It feels like spinning plates half-asleep, with more plates added for good measure. But perfection isn't the goal. You just need to keep showing up and trying.

Those sudden thoughts, "What if I drop her?" or "I'm the worst at this," are way more common than you might think. They don't mean you're falling apart; they mean your brain is handling something new. Often, our minds fixate on worst-case scenarios not because they'll happen, but because you care deeply. Self-doubt isn't a failure; it's proof you're engaged and trying. The trick is not letting these worries control you.

Start managing anxious moments by noticing them as they arise. If your mind is looping a mistake or dread for the next meltdown, try grounding yourself. Practice naming five things you see, four you can touch, three you hear, two you smell, and one you taste. Anchor yourself in the present; it's usually less scary than what's in your head.

Another tool: box breathing. Inhale for four counts, hold for four, exhale for four, hold for four more. Repeat until you feel yourself relax. This calms your nervous system and signals that panic isn't needed.

Consider jotting down a "parent win" at the end of the day, even something small, like remembering an extra onesie or smiling through a rough patch. These victories often vanish in the fog of anxiety, but collecting them shows you're more capable than your inner critic says.

Mistakes will happen, sometimes funny, sometimes awkward, but if you treat them as lessons rather than proof you're failing, they're valuable. The first time I forgot the diaper bag, I dried my kid off with my shirt in a Target bathroom. Embarrassing, sure, but I learned to double-check before leaving the house and keep a spare in the car. Reflect on these moments with, "What did I learn?" instead of, "Why do I suck?" One dad shared he once snapped a onesie over pajamas and only noticed at bedtime. Everyone laughed, and no harm was done.

Expectations can trip you up. Comparing yourself to Instagram dads or impossible standards will only feed anxiety. Instead, write your own "dad job description," what's important to you, not what others expect. Maybe it's "Be present at bedtime" or "Stay patient when things are loud." Your list should be uniquely yours. Great dads aren't perfect; they're real, adaptable, and willing to apologize and restart.

Grab a notebook or your phone and, in a few lines, jot down what matters most to you as a parent, not what your parents did or what social media dictates. Maybe it's raising a kind child or bringing laughter to tough days. Use these as your guiding principles when anxiety sneaks in.

Nobody becomes Superdad overnight, and anyone who says otherwise is exaggerating or forgetting. Your child doesn't need perfect; they need present, honest, and loving. Showing up, even when you mess up, builds trust and resilience in both of you. Allow yourself to be imperfect, laugh off your mistakes, and keep going, even on the worst days.

Anxiety grows in silence. Sharing your worries with another dad or even writing them down reduces their power. Some days will feel chaotic; others will be quieter but heavy with self-doubt. That's part of parenting, not a sign you're not enough.

A year from now, your child won't remember if you folded a swaddle perfectly or did voices in stories just right. What they'll remember is that you were there, imperfect, genuine, loving, which is exactly what "doing it right" looks like.

Building Your Dad Support Squad (Without Forced Small Talk)

I never pictured myself searching for "dad friends," but parenthood has a way of changing social habits. Early on, I thought I could handle everything on my own, but isolation gradually crept in. Most new dads don't imagine themselves joining dad groups or swapping diaper tips in crowded cafes; forced small talk or awkward meetups just feel exhausting, especially if you're an introvert or tired of talking about the weather. Still, finding your people, even in unlikely places, can really lighten those long, draining days.

Support often shows up where you least expect it. Sometimes it's at work, like noticing a tired coworker with spit-up on his shirt and sharing a knowing look. A simple "Rough night?" or a quick chat by the coffee machine can spark a genuine connection without any pressure. Hobbies are another goldmine: fantasy football leagues, BBQ groups, or video game sessions tend to drift from stats to stories about parenting chaos. Online spaces like Reddit's r/daddit or local Facebook groups fill a gap, making it easy to share struggles and advice without face-to-face pressure.

Reaching out doesn't mean baring your soul in a group circle. Low-effort connections work well. Text threads, for instance, let dads swap memes about sleepless nights or share photos of parenting disasters. Humor helps break the ice and reminds you you're not alone. Prefer something a bit more active? Organize a dad-and-baby coffee walk, no deep talks, just caffeine, strollers, and the option to chat as you wander. These low-key hangouts are perfect if you dislike structure but want connection.

If you're nervous about reaching out, start small. You don't have to share your deepest struggles, send a funny meme about new dad life, or drop an article link in a group chat. It's often easier to connect over humor or shared stories than to launch into heavy topics. Gradually, these little check-ins become anchors: a simple "How's everyone's sleep?" or "Anyone else dealing with teething?" often leads to honest, judgment-free replies.

Maintaining these connections doesn't take a lot of effort, even when you're busy. Group chats are a lifesaver: they let you reply on your own time. Set up regular check-ins, maybe Sunday nights, everyone shares a "dad win" from the week, big or small (like surviving a blowout or getting a smile after a rough morning). These small rituals create camaraderie and keep everyone engaged without taking up much time.

Your support squad doesn't need to be big; just two or three dads you trust can make a difference. Swapping tips about bottles or venting about tantrums creates real bonds, sometimes deeper than pre-parent friendships. You'll get advice you didn't know you needed, like how to remove spit-up stains or which parks have the best playgrounds. Helping another dad through a tough moment also boosts your own mood. Perspective doubles when shared.

One night, after my daughter screamed for hours, I sent a panicked message to my group chat: "Is this normal, or do I have a banshee?" Instantly, two dads chimed in with solidarity. One even sent a meme that made me laugh and snap out of my spiral. At the playground, a simple conversation about diaper bags became a regular Saturday meet-up and a lasting friendship. Moments like these don't require emotional speeches or planned events; just showing up however you can is enough.

Your support system might look different; maybe it's your brother, a college friend with twins, or a neighbor you pass on stroller walks. The essential part is openness: share a bit of your real, messy day. Don't wait for someone else to start the conversation; sometimes one honest text or a coffee walk is all it takes to shift from struggling alone to thriving together.

There's no manual for fatherhood, but strength multiplies in numbers, even if it's just two guys swapping memes at midnight while their babies wail. Connection doesn't need scripts or ceremonies; it just needs honesty, willingness to reach out, and maybe even the occasional emoji.

Embracing the Dad Bod: Health, Wellness, and Self-Compassion

The "dad bod," a term often joked about in memes and casual banter, carries pressures of both pride and shame. While the soft edges might spark humor, they're also evidence of late nights, skipped workouts, and meals eaten on the go while juggling parenting. Right now, forget pursuing a six-pack; your real achievement is simply being present for your family in whatever shape you're in.

Redefining fitness as a new dad means dropping the pursuit of perfection. Instead, focus on movement that fits your current life: squats while holding your baby, couch push-ups, hallway lunges during nap time, or stroller "runs" that are sometimes more determined walks. The goal isn't beating old gym records; it's about feeling good and having the energy to keep up with your little one. Leave behind old standards; this is a new chapter with new priorities.

When it comes to eating, the kitchen doesn't have to be a source of stress. Keep it simple: prep snacks like granola bars, cut fruit, and yogurt in batches to avoid less healthy options. Rely on one-pot dinners and slow cooker meals to save time. Planning lunches (even leftovers) prevents slipping into fast food habits that leave you sluggish. If you didn't prep meals before your baby arrived, lean on pre-washed greens, rotisserie chicken, and ready-made grains. Eating well isn't about strict "clean eating," it's about fueling yourself so you can keep going.

Sleep is a major challenge for new dads. Advice to "sleep when the baby sleeps" often feels unhelpful, but every minute counts. Share night shifts with your partner if you can; short naps can be surprisingly restorative. If you're alone, try to nap near your baby or during an afternoon feed. Use a sleep mask for daytime naps, and don't feel guilty for prioritizing rest over chores; no one can function on no sleep for long.

Physical self-care connects directly with your mood and patience. A quick walk after a rough morning can reset your mind. A good meal does more than stop hunger; it can elevate your mood and help with irritability. Your body may have changed, but it's working hard for you each day, and that's worth respecting.

Practicing gratitude towards your body means focusing on what it accomplishes now, not what it did in the past. Maybe you lugged a stroller up the stairs, rocked your baby to sleep for hours, or simply endured another hectic day. These actions display strength. The first time pushing a stroller while running might feel awkward, but those shared moments are what matter, not your speed or style.

Looking in the mirror and appreciating your body's stretch marks, scars, or softness takes courage. These marks record your efforts and care. Instead of chasing a perfect ideal, ask yourself: "What did my body do for me today?" Did you comfort your baby, carry groceries and the car seat, or dance through a tough evening? These small victories mean more than any unattainable standard.

A helpful reflection exercise is to jot down one thing your body accomplished today, even if it was just making it through another sleep-deprived day. These notes become reminders that health is about energy, presence, and resilience, not just appearances.

Ultimately, the "dad bod" is a badge of involvement, showing that your priorities have shifted for the better. You're exchanging gym time for precious moments on the playmat or with bottles at 2 a.m. It might not feel glamorous, but it's true strength.

Physical health as a new dad isn't about achieving perfection. It's about small, sustainable choices, a little grace, and gratitude for what your body achieves day by day. The dad bod isn't a punchline, it's earned, one sleepless night at a time.

Next, we'll talk about tracking your baby's milestones and knowing when to worry, so you can focus your energy where it matters most.

CHAPTER 6
Navigating Milestones and Emergencies: What's Normal, What's Not

Customizable Dad-Friendly Milestone Trackers

The first time I saw my baby grin, it hit me like a lightning bolt, just a gummy, crooked smile that made every sleepless night worth it. I didn't need a book to know it was special, but I did wonder, "Is this early? Late? Should I write this down?" Enter milestone trackers. Not the overwhelming kind, but simple tools you can actually use without guilt if you miss a few boxes or dates. Your baby doesn't care about perfect checklists; they care about you cheering them on.

Let's break milestones down by month, but remember: "normal" covers a wide range. Some babies roll over at three months, others at five. Some babble at six months, others wait until nine to say their first "da-da." The CDC and other sources highlight these windows for good reason: babies aren't robots on the same timeline. Key first-year milestones generally include: first real smile (6–8 weeks), holding eye contact (by 2 months), rolling from tummy to back (around 4 months), big laughs or babbling (4–6 months), sitting up with support (6 months), crawling/scooting (8–10 months), standing with help, and those first wobbly steps by one year. Every milestone has an early, average, and late window. Some babies skip crawling and jump straight to walking, while others focus on fine motor skills before saying "mama."

Every month, jot down what stands out, even if it isn't in a baby book. Maybe your highlight is that first moment of eye contact or a funny little wiggle you won't find on any milestone chart. You decide what's important. I encourage you to create your own tracker. A one-page sheet on your fridge or a note in your phone is perfect. Enter the classic markers for each month: smile (6–8 weeks), eye contact (2 months), rolling (4 months), laughing (4–5 months), babbling (6 months), sitting (6–7 months), crawling (8–10 months), pulling to stand (9–12 months), first steps (anytime between 9–18 months). Next to each, leave a "Dad Win" space for your own memorable moments, even if it's just "Slept through (sort of)," or "Made her giggle with my goofy dance moves."

If it feels like your baby is behind, don't panic. Every milestone has its own range, and being late doesn't always mean something is wrong. If your baby isn't rolling at five months but seems alert, that's often fine. If they sit up at nine months instead of six but are progressing in other areas, that's likely still normal. Delays are only worrisome with other red flags: sudden loss of skills, extreme stiffness/floppiness, no social smiles or eye contact by four months, or total silence and no gestures by ten months. In such cases, contact your pediatrician and trust your instincts; you know your child best. Otherwise, relax and focus on steady progress instead of dates.

Comparison is a trap. Social media makes it seem like every baby is sprinting ahead, but you rarely see the struggles and delays behind the scenes. Celebrate each little step with pride, whether it's a first giggle, stubborn crawl, or your own success at changing a diaper without disaster.

Dad Milestone Reflection Prompt

At the end of each month, spend a few minutes filling this in: "Proud moment of the month:________________________"

It can be any little win: a new skill, a silly face, or just surviving a tough week together.

Take a photo, jot a note on your phone, or share it with your partner. These moments add up quickly and tell the real story of your first year as a dad.

Remember, this year isn't about perfect timing; it's about being present for the big and small moments unique to your child's journey. Your baby needs you to show up and cheer them on, no matter their individual timeline.

Red Flags and Real Emergencies: Dad's Guide to Baby Health

Every parent eventually faces that moment of panic: a strange rash, an unsettling cough, or a high fever. Deciding whether to shrug it off, call the pediatrician, or rush to the ER can feel overwhelming. A simple green, yellow, red system can help. Green means "don't panic," for minor sniffles, mild spit-up, or a harmless rash. Yellow means "be alert," for a low-grade fever, unusual fussiness, or odd-looking poop, but your baby is still mostly acting normal. Red means "take action now," for high fevers, especially in babies under three months, labored breathing with ribs pulling in, grunting, or flared nostrils, blue lips, ongoing vomiting, or seizures. Eating problems, like refusing two feeds in a row or having no wet diapers for eight hours, also warrant a call. Watch for sudden limpness, a bulging soft spot on the head, or a rash that doesn't blanch when pressed.

Emergencies can hit in the middle of the night and make you question everything. For babies under three months with a fever over 100.4°F/38°C, call your doctor immediately. For older babies, consider both the number and behavior. If they're hard to wake, extremely irritable, wheezing, or refusing fluids, seek help. Breathing issues are serious; if you see blue lips, retractions, grunting, or head bobbing, call 911 or go to the ER. Vomiting is usually manageable, but becomes urgent if it's projectile, recurring, or contains blood or green bile. Any seizure, shaking, or loss of consciousness requires immediate care.

Here are quick responses to common emergencies:

- **High fever**: Use a rectal thermometer, keep the baby lightly dressed, offer fluids, monitor for other symptoms (rash, stiff neck, odd cry). Call the doctor right away if under three months; call if there are additional red flag symptoms in older babies.

- **Breathing trouble**: Check for chest retractions, stridor (high-pitched wheeze), or if your baby is too breathless to feed. Keep your baby upright and call emergency services.

- **Non-stop vomiting**: Watch for dehydration: dry mouth, absent tears, no wet diapers. Offer small sips of oral rehydration solution; contact your pediatrician.

- **Seizures**: Lay your baby safely on their side, don't put anything in their mouth, time the episode if you can, and call 911.

Communicating clearly during emergencies helps healthcare providers respond quickly. Start with your baby's age and core symptoms: "I have a 2-month-old with a 101°F fever, who won't wake for feeds." Explain how long it's been happening, what you've tried, and all symptoms, e.g., "She has a red rash on her legs that doesn't fade when pressed." The more specific, the better.

Use a script: "Hi, I'm calling about my [baby's age]. [Symptom] started [when], now she's also [other symptoms]. [Number] wet diapers in [hours], and I'm worried because [reason]." Take notes on their instructions and repeat them back.

From my rookie parent days: One night, I saw purple spots on my daughter's legs and panicked, fearing the worst. At urgent care, the doctor calmly diagnosed a harmless newborn rash, and it disappeared by morning. Moral: It's okay to overreact when you're unsure, especially at first. Keeping a record of vitals (temperature, diaper counts) and focusing on breathing helped me stay calm until we saw a doctor.

Staying level-headed in emergencies is tough, but it is possible. Take three big breaths before acting. Focus on measurable facts: temperature, color, breathing patterns, and diapers. Ask for help. Healthcare providers would much rather reassure you than have you go it alone. Save emergency contacts in your phone, and jot down key details when things are calm so you're ready. Overreact once or twice? That just means you care and are ready for real emergencies when they come.

When Baby Won't Eat, Sleep, or Stop Crying: Troubleshooting

Picture this: it's the middle of the night, you're holding a red-faced, wailing baby and wondering how someone so small can produce that much noise. Whether it's feeding refusal, epic sleep struggles, or a meltdown that just won't quit, every dad hits this wall sooner or later. Instead of letting panic take the wheel, you can break these moments down with clear, step-by-step logic. Think of it as your "dad decision tree." This isn't about being perfect; it's about staying calm and figuring out what's actually going on, one step at a time.

Start with feeding refusal. If your baby turns away from the bottle or breast or outright refuses to eat, pause before going into fix-it mode. Sometimes, babies just aren't hungry yet. First, check for obvious issues: is your baby too sleepy? Try waking with a gentle diaper change or undressing down to the diaper for a bit of cool air. Next, inspect the feeding equipment. Sometimes the bottle nipple gets clogged or the milk temperature is off. If breastfeeding, see if a different position helps or if there's a latch problem (cracked nipples, dribbling milk, or clicking sounds are clues). If your baby is fussy but alert and peeing as usual, try again in 30 minutes. A stuffy nose can make sucking hard; use a bulb syringe or saline drops if needed. If your baby skips more than two feeds in a row or seems listless, call your pediatrician.

Now for sleep struggles: your baby's eyes are wide open at 2 a.m., or they doze off only to wake howling minutes later. First question, hungry? Try a feed, especially if it has been over two hours. Not hungry? Check the diaper. Still fussing? Is the room too hot or cold? Adjust layers and try again. Next, look for gas. Burp gently or cycle their legs like a slow-motion bicycle. White noise machines or apps (even just a running fan) can sometimes settle overstimulated babies. Avoid rocking all night or letting them nap in unsafe places (like car seats outside the car), even if it's tempting in exhaustion. Resist the urge to overfeed just to get more sleep; babies spit up more when overfull.

When crying is the main event and nothing soothes them, it's time to go step by step. Start with the basics: hunger, diaper, temperature. Move to burping and gentle movement (walks, rocking). Try changing scenery. Take your baby to a different room or stand by a window. Dimming the lights and lowering noise levels helps overstimulated little ones settle down. For some, a pacifier works wonders; for others, swaddling (if safe and the baby isn't rolling yet) can calm frazzled nerves. If all else fails, skin-to-skin time might help both of you relax.

Common mistakes crop up in these moments. It's easy to overfeed in hopes of silencing cries. Resist the urge unless you're sure hunger is the issue. Don't layer on extra sleep props like loose blankets or stuffed animals; they're unsafe for babies under one year old. Avoid panicking over normal newborn fussiness. Some babies simply cry more than others, especially in the evenings (a phase often called "the witching hour"). Myths like "letting them cry strengthens their lungs" are outdated. Babies need comfort and support, not tough love, at this age.

Knowing when to call for backup is key. If you've run your troubleshooting checklist, fed, changed, burped, checked temperature and environment, and your baby is still inconsolable after two hours or shows new symptoms (fever, vomiting, limpness, trouble breathing), it's time to reach out. Your partner should always be in the loop; sometimes just swapping shifts and getting fresh eyes on the situation makes all the difference. Don't hesitate to call your pediatrician if your gut says something's off. For crying specifically, most healthy newborns cry up to three hours a day (yes, really), but if it seems excessive or you're getting worried about dehydration (no wet diapers in 6–8 hours), medical advice is a good move.

The real secret is learning to trust yourself and this logical flow: Is my baby hungry? No? Wet? No? Gassy? Tried burping? Too hot/cold? Environment overstimulating? If you've checked every box and still feel lost, that's normal too; it happens to everyone at some point. Taking a break (putting baby safely in their crib and stepping away for five minutes) is not only okay, it's sometimes necessary for your own sanity. Remember, you're not alone on those tough nights; every dad has faced down a marathon cry session and come out on the other side with new skills (and maybe a few more gray hairs). The more you follow these steps, the easier it gets to spot what works for your unique kid, and your confidence will build right alongside theirs.

Sleep Regression Survival: Why It Happens and What to Do

There's a night when you're certain you've cracked the code. Your baby falls asleep early, stays down for a few glorious hours, and you start to believe the worst is over. Then, out of nowhere, your champion sleeper transforms into a pint-sized insomniac, waking every hour, wailing for reasons that seem to change by the minute. If you've hit this wall, you might be smack in the middle of a sleep regression. A phase when your baby's sleep takes a nosedive just as you were getting comfortable. Sleep regressions are notorious for showing up at predictable times: around four months, again at eight months, and another wave near the first birthday. They're not random; they tend to coincide with rapid brain growth, learning new tricks (like rolling or standing), or when separation anxiety kicks in and your baby suddenly needs to check that you haven't disappeared into an alternate dimension every 25 minutes.

Understanding why these regressions happen actually helps. During the four-month regression, your baby's sleep pattern matures and becomes more like an adult's, with lighter sleep cycles and frequent waking. At eight months, crawling, pulling up, and growing curiosity mean brains are busy even at midnight. The twelve-month phase often overlaps with walking and a big burst in language, as babies want to practice their new skills at any hour. It's not bad parenting or something you did; it's biology and development doing their thing. This doesn't make it less exhausting, but at least you know there's a reason behind the chaos.

When you're in the thick of regression nights, routines become your anchor. Stick to a consistent bedtime routine: bath, pajamas, favorite book or song, dim lights. Babies thrive on repetition; the predictability signals that sleep is coming, even if they fight it.

If your baby wakes often, keep interactions boring and calm. No bright lights, no wild games, just soothing whispers and gentle pats. Swapping "night duty" with your partner can save your sanity; take turns or split the night into shifts so both of you get some rest. Tag-teaming isn't just practical; it keeps resentment from building up in the darkness.

Try comfort objects if your baby is old enough (a soft blanket or safe lovey), white noise for blocking out distracting sounds, and keep the crib clear of clutter. If your baby wants to practice standing or crawling in the crib, give them plenty of floor time during the day to burn off that energy.

Surviving these nights takes more than strategy; it takes grit and a willingness to let go of perfect expectations. You'll feel frustration boiling over sometimes. You'll question whether you're doing something wrong. It's normal to look in the mirror and think, *"How do people survive this?"*

The emotional punch of sleep deprivation is real: short tempers, blank stares, sometimes even tears at 3 a.m. Remind yourself: every dad has watched the clock crawl through the early hours and felt like he's failing. This doesn't mean you're weak; it means you care.

Lower your standards for a while; if everyone is fed and safe, that's enough. Keep humor close by. Share "Team No Sleep" war stories with other dads. Text a friend who gets it or scroll through those tired dad memes on your phone at 4 a.m. Sometimes just knowing you're not alone makes those long nights feel less soul-crushing.

Of course, there are moments when sleep issues cross the line from normal regression into something that needs attention. Trust your gut if you see extreme lethargy, your baby can't stay awake for feeds or playtime, or if breathing seems labored or noisy beyond regular newborn sounds. If your child refuses all food and liquids for more than eight hours or has fewer than three wet diapers in 24 hours during these phases, call your doctor. Pay close attention to high fevers or any sign your baby is struggling to breathe comfortably while lying down. These aren't just bumps on the sleep regression road; they're signals that call for professional advice. Don't wait and wonder; reach out for help.

Sleep regressions can feel like a never-ending loop of "why won't you just sleep?" followed by coffee-fueled mornings where you wonder if you'll ever think straight again. The truth is, these phases eventually pass, even if it feels impossible in the moment. Every time you get through a rough night, you're building resilience, not just for your baby but for yourself too. You learn to adapt, improvise, and find small victories where you can, like celebrating a two-hour stretch of unbroken sleep as if you've won an award.

This isn't about being superhuman; it's about hanging on, together, until the storm passes and a new stage begins.

Tummy Time and Development: Making It Work (Even with Protests)

Tummy time sounds simple, but if you're like most new dads, the first time you put your baby on their stomach, you get a lot of protest and a face that says, "Why are you doing this to me?"

Here's the thing: tummy time is way more than a baby workout. It's a daily boost for your kid's physical and brain growth. When your little one pushes up on their arms, even for a few seconds, they're building neck strength, shoulder stability, and the core muscles that set the stage for rolling, crawling, and eventually walking. Plus, spending time on their tummy helps prevent those flat spots on the back of the head that come from too much lying down. It also encourages visual tracking and hand coordination. Your baby learns to reach, bat at toys, and eventually scoot toward something interesting. Cognitive skills get a boost too, because every wobbly push-up is a lesson in cause and effect.

Doctors say you should aim for tummy time from day one, just a minute or two at first, working up to about an hour total by three months old. Don't worry; your baby doesn't have to do it all at once. You can break it up into lots of short sessions throughout the day. Think of it as practice, not a test. Your lap counts. Lying on your chest counts. Even propping your baby up over your arm while you watch TV together is fair game. The main thing is to make it a habit and keep adding a little more each week.

If you want to make it fun (or at least less terrible), try mixing things up. Babies love faces more than anything. Get down at their level and smile, make funny noises, or stick out your tongue. Try using mirrors; most babies are fascinated by their own reflection (and if you're honest, it's kind of hilarious seeing that confused stare). Bring in favorite toys or bright rattles and place them just out of reach to encourage reaching and swiping. Sometimes what works best is the old-school move: lean back on the couch with your shirt off and put your baby belly-down on your chest. That skin-to-skin time counts as tummy time and feels safe for both of you. And if your baby fusses after ten seconds, that's completely normal. Pick them up, give them a break, then try again later.

Of course, not every session goes smoothly. Some babies seem to hate tummy time with a passion. They'll cry, flip over, or just bury their face and refuse to move. This isn't a sign you're doing things wrong; some kids resist because it feels strange or hard at first. If your baby rolls right over or fusses nonstop, don't take it personally. You can try singing their favorite silly song or narrating what you see: "Whoa! You're so strong!" Sometimes joining them on the floor does the trick. Lie down right beside your baby so they feel like they have company in the struggle. Try moving them to different rooms or changing up the scenery with soft blankets or patterned mats.

Keep sessions short if needed; two to three minutes is fine to start. Gradually add a bit more time as your baby gets stronger and more comfortable. Celebrate every win: that first time they lift their head for longer than five seconds; the moment they prop up on elbows instead of face-planting; that hesitant kick that finally rolls them onto their back. Each bit of progress is worth cheering about.

Here's a dad hack that actually helps: keep a log or chart, nothing fancy; even tally marks on your fridge work. Write down how many minutes your baby spends each day on their tummy and what new moves you spot. Did they push up higher this week? Did they finally reach for that stuffed giraffe? Snap photos if you want; a quick before-and-after series can show how far you've both come in just a few weeks.

Some of my proudest moments as a dad happened during these sessions, not just because my kid got better at tummy time, but because I was there cheering him on, clapping like a fool when he finally found his balance. You'll have days when your baby screams through the whole thing and days when they surprise you with sudden strength or curiosity. It's all progress, even the messy, noisy parts count.

The key is to stay patient and flexible. If today's session is a disaster, try again later or switch up your approach. If you're consistent (and forgiving), your baby will grow stronger and more confident, and you'll rack up those "dad win" moments that make all the difference in these early months.

Vaccines, Checkups, and What to Actually Worry About

Staying on top of vaccines and checkups is one of those things that sounds simple on paper but always feels like a logistical puzzle in real life. The baby's first year is jam-packed with appointments, each with its own set of shots and questions. If you're like most new dads, you want to know what's coming up and how to make those doctor visits less of an ordeal for everyone involved. Let's break it down so you can show up ready, not scrambling.

The first-year vaccine schedule is pretty standard, and most pediatricians will hand you a printout, but it helps to have a dad-specific cheat sheet. At birth, your baby gets the first dose of Hepatitis B (usually right in the hospital). At two months, expect a flurry: DTaP (diphtheria, tetanus, pertussis), Polio, Hib (Haemophilus influenzae type b), PCV13 (pneumococcal), and Rotavirus. Four months brings repeat doses of all these except Hep B. Six months is similar, another round of DTaP, Polio, Hib, PCV13, Hep B, and Rotavirus. Around twelve months, it's time for MMR (measles, mumps, rubella), Varicella (chickenpox), Hepatitis A, and another PCV13 shot. If you're a checklist person, print this out or set reminders on your phone. Add the date and jot down any reactions or questions after each visit.

Knowing what's routine at each visit helps you relax before the appointment. Most checkups involve measuring weight and length, getting a head circumference, checking reflexes, and talking about feeding, sleep, and milestones. Your doctor will often ask about what your baby is doing: rolling over, grabbing toys, babbling, or making eye contact. Sometimes it feels like a pop quiz on your own kid. Don't stress if you can't remember every detail; bring notes or even videos if you want to highlight something new (or weird) you've noticed.

When it comes to vaccines, most babies will have some mild side effects, maybe a little fever (under 101°F), some crankiness, more sleepiness than usual, or swelling at the shot site. These are normal and usually clear up in a day or two. A cool washcloth or baby-safe pain reliever (if approved by your doc) can help. What's not normal is a persistent high fever (over 103°F), swelling that keeps getting worse or turns hard and red, trouble breathing, or extreme listlessness after shots. If you see any of these red flags, call your pediatrician right away.

Advocating for your kid at these appointments doesn't mean grilling your doctor on every detail, but don't hold back if something feels off or you're just confused. It's totally fine to say, "I'm worried about this rash," or "He doesn't make eye contact like other babies at daycare, is that okay?" Some good questions for your toolkit:

- "Is this delay in rolling, sitting, or whatever milestone— something I should worry about?"

- "How can I make recovery easier for my partner after delivery or surgery?"

- "Are there ways to make shots less stressful for my baby?"

- "If I notice [symptom], should I call right away or just watch it?"

If you forget what you meant to ask by the time the doctor walks in (it happens to all of us), keep a running note on your phone or use a sticky note in the diaper bag. Jot down anything weird or new during the week, odd poops, new habits, feeding quirks, so your mind doesn't go blank when the pediatrician looks at you.

Doctor visits are smoother with a little prep work. Pack a "doctor bag" before leaving: favorite small toy or pacifier (distraction is everything), feeding supplies (bottle or snack if age-appropriate), and don't forget a snack for yourself. Those waits can drag on. Bring an extra onesie in case of diaper disasters and a thin blanket for comfort in chilly offices. If your baby gets fussy post-shots, gentle rocking, a quick feed if allowed, or some silly faces can help calm things down. Sometimes just stepping outside for a minute after the appointment resets everyone's mood.

No two babies react the same way to checkups. Some take shots in stride; others act like it's the end of the world. Either way, try not to overthink it if you have a rough day at the clinic. You're not being judged on how calm or composed your kid is. You're there to keep them healthy and safe, and that's what counts.

Chapter Wrap-Up

Getting through all these health checks and vaccines isn't just about checking boxes; it's about being present, asking questions, and knowing when to push for more help. You've got what it takes to advocate for your child and support your partner through all the pokes and paperwork. Up next: balancing work demands with family life, because being there for your baby means figuring out how to juggle it all without losing yourself in the process.

CHAPTER 7
Work-Life Balance: Staying Present at Home and Work

Designing Your "Morning Launchpad" Routine

Mornings used to be simple: alarm, shower, coffee, out the door. Now, they can feel chaotic, you're juggling a baby, scanning work emails, chasing essentials, and navigating last-minute messes (like the cat's hallway surprise). This might not be the morning you imagined, but it's reality for many new dads.

You can't erase all the morning chaos, but you can make it manageable with a personalized routine. The key is to prioritize what's truly essential and skip the rest. Draw a line between what must get done, like changing the baby, prepping bottles, packing the diaper bag, and what can wait, such as ironing your shirt or scrolling through Instagram. Keep your essentials list short: feed, change and dress baby, pack the bag, and gather your wallet, keys, and work badge. Anything beyond that is optional.

Efficiency doesn't mean sacrificing connection. Simple morning rituals can turn routines into bonding opportunities. For some, it's a quick "family snuggle" or a two-minute dance party with the kids. It doesn't have to be complex; the magic is in its consistency. A kiss for your partner or a silly song for your child can transform a frantic morning into a shared moment.

Preparing the night before is your best strategy for calmer mornings. Set out clothes for everyone, no early-morning digging for clean onesies. Prep bottles and snacks ahead; organize them in the fridge or by the door. Make sure the diaper bag has spare outfits and wipes (always pack a second onesie), and get your work bag ready, laptop, charger, headphones, whatever you need, so you're not scavenging through the house before your coffee kicks in.

On the topic of coffee, a programmable coffee maker is a lifesaver. Set it to brew before you get up so you're lured from bed by fresh coffee aroma. For breakfast, prep grab-and-go options like overnight oats or egg muffins, easy to eat while managing a baby.

A dedicated "launchpad zone" at home streamlines departures. Whether it's a table by the door or a hallway shelf, give every essential a spot: bags, lunches, keys, water bottles, shoes. Keep a checklist handy if you're forgetful: "Diaper bag? Bottles? Coffee? Baby's toy?" A bit of organization upfront prevents headaches later.

Don't rush the morning handoff, whether it's to your partner, daycare, or a grandparent. Make these goodbyes meaningful, with a quick rhyme, secret handshake, or note—simple routines remind your child and partner they matter, even in the rush. For your partner, pause for a quick check-in: "Need anything from me?" or "Let's crush it today." These small moments build connection and teamwork.

Interactive Element: Morning Launchpad Checklist

- Set out tomorrow's clothes for everyone.

- Prep bottles/snacks and stash in fridge.

- Pack diaper bag with two outfits, wipes, and a pacifier.

- Load work bag with essentials.

- Place both bags in the launchpad zone near the door.

- Set the coffee maker timer.

- Write a quick checklist or reminder note.

- Decide on a morning ritual—a dance party, snuggle, or high-five.

Try this checklist for one week and adjust as needed until your mornings feel smoother.

By organizing and making space for quick moments of connection, you'll reduce the frantic searches, avoid forgotten items, and set everyone up for a better day.

Staying Connected After Paternity Leave

Returning to work after paternity leave can feel like a collision of two worlds. One minute, you're the go-to person for midnight feedings, baby burps, and surprise diaper blowouts. Next, you're back in meetings, emails, and lunchroom small talk, feeling like you've left half your heart at home.

Most dads I've talked to describe that first week back as a strange mix of relief, guilt, and sadness. You might even feel invisible; some coworkers are eager to hear "dad stories," but the pace of work hasn't slowed down for your adjustment. The anxiety is real: *Am I missing too much? Will my partner resent me for being out of the house? How do I stay involved when I'm not physically there?*

It's normal to miss your baby with a deep ache and still crave adult conversation and a break from baby talk. That doesn't make you a bad dad; it makes you human. One friend told me he spent his first lunch break hiding in his car, scrolling through baby photos and wondering if the baby would even remember him by the end of the week. Another dad confessed that seeing photos of his partner's "perfect" day on social media left him feeling left out and weirdly competitive, like he was missing the magic moments. These feelings often come in waves: pride for working hard, guilt for not being home, relief for small freedoms, and longing for baby snuggles.

Staying connected during the workday takes a little creativity. Scheduled photo or video updates are a simple way to bridge the gap. Ask your partner or caregiver to send you a daily pic or short clip, maybe after nap time or during lunch. Set an alarm as a reminder if needed. Even ten seconds of seeing your baby's face can reset your mood and remind you what you're working for. If your workplace allows it, take a lunch break and FaceTime or make a quick call home. It doesn't need to be long; even a minute or two can help you feel involved and let your partner know you're thinking about them. Some dads use their commute for voice memos, recording a silly message or song to be played for the baby later.

Advocating for flexibility at work might feel intimidating at first, but it's worth considering if your job allows any wiggle room. If you want to request remote days, flexible start times, or a phased return, plan what you'll say in advance. Here's an example: "I've really valued my time at home with my new child. To stay focused and productive at work while still supporting my family, I'd like to discuss the possibility of working from home one day a week (or adjusting my hours temporarily). I'm committed to meeting my responsibilities and believe this change will help me bring my best self to both roles." Most managers appreciate honest communication and clear plans. If remote work isn't possible, see if you can adjust your hours slightly to avoid traffic and maximize morning or evening family time.

Walking in the door after a long day can set the mood for your whole evening. It's easy to get sucked into checking messages or zoning out as soon as you drop your bag, but a quick "tech-off" ritual helps shift gears from work brain to dad brain. Try leaving your phone in another room for twenty minutes when you get home—just enough time to focus on your family before catching up on notifications. If you've had a particularly stressful day, take a five-minute decompression walk around the block or even just stand outside and take a few breaths before heading inside. This small pause can make you less snappy and more present.

Make the first moments at home count. Instead of rushing straight to chores or screens, greet your baby and partner with intention, maybe it's a "first hug goes to baby" rule or a silly "I'm home!" song that makes everyone laugh. Let your partner know you see them with eye contact and a genuine question about their day before diving into logistics or complaints. These habits tell your family they matter more than any lingering work stress.

Balancing work and family isn't about perfection; it's about showing up where you are, with whatever energy you have left. If you can't be physically present during the day, small actions keep you emotionally connected. Celebrate the wins: that lunch break video call, the silly voice memo, or the moment when your baby lights up at your arrival, even if it's just for ten minutes before dinner chaos begins. Your presence, even in these micro-bursts, shapes your bond more than any grand gesture. Over time, these rituals become anchors for both you and your family—reminders that while work is important, being present matters most.

There's no blueprint for finding equilibrium here. Every family is different, and every workplace has its quirks. But each intentional act, requesting flexibility, prioritizing connection over distraction, protecting those first moments at home, adds up. The days are busy and sometimes messy, but these choices help keep you right where you want to be: in the center of your child's life, even when you're pulled in every direction.

Maximizing Family Time in 10-Minute Windows

You might think you need whole afternoons or a free weekend to really connect with your baby, but real life rarely hands you those wide-open spaces. It's the micro-moments, the in-between slices of your day, that add up. Research on child development keeps coming back to this: kids thrive on quality, not just quantity. Your baby doesn't care how flashy the moment is; what matters most is your attention, even if it's just for ten focused minutes. The myth that only hours-long playdates build memories just isn't true. Those pint-sized bursts of connection, where you're engaged, present, and available, are the building blocks of trust and attachment.

Imagine you're home after work with a list of chores and a baby who's grumpy after a short nap. Instead of stressing about not having an hour to spare, look for your ten-minute window. Maybe you scoop up your little one, flop onto the living room rug, and start a silly sing-along. Your baby might not understand every word, but the rhythm, the sound of your voice, and the goofy faces will light them up. Or grab a board book and let your kid "help" turn the pages, making animal sounds at every picture. It's less about finishing the story and more about that shared laugh when you both moo like cows or roar like dinosaurs.

If you want a menu of ten-minute dad-and-baby activities to keep handy, here's a quick list: have a sock puppet storytime with two mismatched socks and some wild voices; shake out the wiggles with a morning dance party; crank up your favorite song and bounce around together; take a stroller or carrier stroll around the block, even if it's just to the corner and back; invent a silly face contest in front of the mirror, seeing who can make the baby giggle first; or hold an impromptu "parade" through the house banging wooden spoons on pots. You don't need fancy toys or Pinterest-worthy crafts to make magic. Your energy, even if you're tired, is what turns routine moments into memories.

Protecting these micro-windows in your day takes intention, but it's possible even on busy schedules. Block out ten minutes on your phone calendar and label it "Baby Break." Treat it like any other meeting. Set a recurring reminder for right after dinner or before bedtime so this time doesn't get swallowed by chores or screens. If you work from home or have odd hours, sandwich these moments between calls or emails—take a stretch break and roll a ball back and forth on the floor or play peekaboo behind your laptop. The trick isn't to find more time but to use what you have with total focus, no multitasking.

Sometimes the urge to check your phone creeps in, but resist it during these ten-minute bursts. Let notifications wait. Give your kid your eyes and your hands for just those minutes. Babies and toddlers are pros at sensing when you're only half-present. They want all of you, even for just one silly little block of time. That attention means more than any expensive gadget could.

If you're worried about not remembering these moments or want to see how they add up over time, consider starting a "Dad Win" mini-journal or photo log. After each micro-activity, snap a quick selfie with your kid—maybe both of you covered in drool after raspberry blowing or sporting wild hair from dance time. These photos become proof that connection isn't about perfection; it's about presence. If journaling feels daunting, keep it simple: jot down one sentence each night describing your favorite mini-moment from the day ("Today we played monster parade in the kitchen, and baby shrieked with laughter"). Some dads share their high point and low point of the day with their partner after bedtime, a quick check-in that makes both of you feel seen.

The power of reflection can't be overstated here. Looking back at your mini-journal or scrolling through those goofy selfies will remind you that even during weeks packed with work stress or sleepless nights, you found time for joy. You built connection in small doses, ten minutes at a time. There's no scorecard for who did it best, but there's immense value in knowing these micro-moments are shaping your child's sense of security and their view of you as present and loving.

The beauty of these short windows is that they're flexible. If one day goes sideways and you miss your moment, just find another tomorrow. No guilt required. You're teaching your child that love doesn't wait for big events, it lives in the quick, everyday bursts that fill their world with laughter and safety.

Dad Guilt: Letting Go of Perfection and Comparison

Dad guilt creeps in quietly. You think you're just tired from work, but suddenly you catch yourself wondering if you're doing enough—at home, with your kid, for your partner. Maybe you scrolled past a post of a dad baking homemade muffins after running a half marathon and helping with math homework, all before noon. It's ridiculous, yet you feel a pang in your chest. Why can't I keep up? Social media is a highlight reel and, let's be honest, nobody posts about the nights they lost it or served frozen pizza three days in a row. Still, the pressure is real. Everyone seems to be winning at this dad thing, except you, right? It's easy to believe the myth of the "super-parent," that you should always be productive, patient, and perfectly present, no matter what.

Cultural expectations pile on top. There's this unspoken script that says you should be crushing it at work while also being emotionally tuned in, physically present, and always available at home. Cue the guilt when you fall short in either direction. Miss a bedtime because of late meetings? Guilt. Snap at your partner after a long day? More guilt. And when tension builds between work deadlines and family needs, you end up feeling like you're failing everywhere—never quite enough anywhere. That's the mental trap so many dads fall into: thinking you're the only one who drops the ball sometimes.

The first thing that helps is recognizing when unrealistic standards have snuck in. Sometimes it takes stepping back for a reality check. Here's an exercise that works: Write down what's actually in your control today and what isn't. You can't control the baby's sleep schedule or surprise work emergencies. You can control how you respond to stress or if you say yes to another project when your plate is full. Ask yourself, *"What would I tell my best friend if he was in my shoes?"* Odds are, you'd give him a break, remind him he's doing his best, and maybe even crack a joke about survival being enough some days.

There's real freedom in picking your battles, choosing what matters most right now, and letting the rest slide without shame. On days when everything feels like too much, focus on just three things that are most important. Maybe it's making your baby laugh, having a real conversation with your partner, and finishing that urgent work task. Circle those three and let everything else, the dishes, unread emails, over-the-top playdates, sit on the back burner for now. This isn't laziness; it's survival with intention. When someone asks for help or an invitation pops up, try saying, "I can't this time," or "Not today." No explanation required. Protecting your bandwidth is self-care.

Here's something I wish every new dad could see: Even the days that go sideways can still be good ones. There was this one Thursday when nothing went according to plan. The baby woke screaming from a nap just as I dialed into a meeting. Lunch turned into a handful of crackers scavenged between diaper changes and spilled milk. My partner and I snapped at each other over whose turn it was to take out the trash. I felt like I'd lost at both work and home before 2 p.m.

But then, while sitting on the floor in mismatched socks and a stained shirt, I started making faces at my daughter just to break the tension. She cracked up, drool running down her chin, and suddenly, everything else faded out for a minute. That laugh didn't erase my stress or magically finish my to-do list, but it mattered more than any perfect plan.

Some of my favorite memories as a dad didn't look impressive from the outside. They weren't Instagram-worthy: just me and my son sitting on the porch in the rain, sharing soggy crackers; me letting my kid "help" fold laundry by wearing every sock on his arms; watching cartoons together when I was too fried to play pretend. Those moments felt real, imperfect but honest. They're the ones I remember most when I'm tempted to measure myself against someone else's filtered story.

Dad guilt loves to whisper that you're not enough unless you juggle everything flawlessly. That's not true. Your kid cares about how you show up, not what you get done or how others see it. If all you can do some days is be there, even if tired or distracted, you're still enough. Permission granted to drop the cape, skip perfection, and just be present for the mess and magic alike.

Managing Work Stress Without Bringing It Home

Work stress is sneaky. It follows you, clings to your shoulders like an invisible backpack, and before you know it, that pressure from the day seeps into your life at home. You might notice you're short-tempered as soon as you walk through the door, snapping at your partner over nothing, rolling your eyes at the baby's fuss, or feeling totally checked out even when you're sitting right there on the living room floor. Sometimes it's not obvious at first. Maybe you find yourself staring off into space, not really hearing the questions your partner asks, or scrolling through your phone while your kid tugs on your pant leg. Mood shifts can be subtle: a sigh that's a little too heavy, a one-word answer where you'd usually tell a story, or that feeling of being stuck in two places at once—your body at home, your mind still tangled in emails and deadlines.

The trouble is, if you let that stress tag along every day, it builds up. Suddenly, small annoyances explode into arguments over who forgot to buy wipes or whose turn it is to handle bedtime. You might start feeling like you're failing as a dad or partner, when really, you're just carrying too much from work into the house. The first trick is spotting the early signs: irritability right after getting home, zoning out during dinner, or feeling waves of frustration out of proportion to what's actually happening. If you start to feel like the world's worst version of yourself for no apparent reason, pause and check if work followed you home.

Transition rituals help break this spell. Think of them as a mental "costume change." Even if you work from home, it makes a difference. Change into comfy clothes as soon as you clock out; the physical swap signals your brain it's time to shift gears. If you commute by car or train, take five slow breaths before walking inside—inhale for four seconds, exhale for six, let your mind clear for just a moment. Some dads swear by walking around the block before entering the house, using the time to shake off meetings and reset their focus. If you're coming from a stressful day in the kitchen, bathroom, or bedroom "office," close your laptop with intention, stand up, stretch, and shake it off for sixty seconds before stepping back into family mode.

Talking about work stress with your partner is vital, but there's a fine line between healthy sharing and letting it flood the evening. The "headline and feelings" method works wonders: give a quick summary like "Tough day, boss dumped a new project on me," then add how you feel about it, "I'm annoyed but glad to be done." Then move on. This way, your partner knows what's going on without feeling like they have to fix it or absorb all of your stress. Set boundaries for venting: maybe agree on five or ten minutes of "work talk," then switch topics. If you find yourself spiraling or getting heated again later in the night, remind yourself, "Headline only," and save the deep dive for another time or a different friend who gets the grind.

Self-compassion is key here. Some days will be rough; that doesn't make you a bad dad. Quick stress reduction practices can do wonders and don't require carving out a whole hour alone. Family walks after dinner are simple but powerful—moving together gets everyone fresh air and burns off leftover tension from the day. Don't underestimate the power of a short gratitude roundtable at dinner: each person (even if it's just you and your partner) shares one thing that went well or made them smile. This isn't about pretending everything's perfect; it's about rewiring your brain to see good moments even in messy days.

One of my favorite tricks is what I call the "3-minute driveway reset." Before I step inside, whether I'm coming home from work or just done with chores, I sit in the car with no music and no phone. I roll my shoulders back, take three deep breaths, and remind myself that whatever happened at work stays outside those walls. Sometimes I picture myself leaving all my stress in the glove compartment. Then I go inside, ready to greet my family as dad, not as an overworked employee.

All these strategies take practice. You'll mess up sometimes, you'll still bark at someone or zone out mid-conversation, but having these small rituals in place gives you a way back to center. When you show up, present and unburdened (or at least trying), everyone feels it. Your kid doesn't need perfection; they need to see you make the effort to be there with them, even when work has been brutal. That effort, those transition moments, those resets, matter more than any grand gesture or apology later on.

The Dad and Partner Check-In: Keeping Your Team Strong

Relationships in the first year after a baby arrives are tested in ways few expect. It's not just sleepless nights or endless chores; it's the subtle disconnect that can happen as you both power through survival mode. Regular check-ins with your partner are essential to prevent drifting apart. These aren't exhaustive problem-solving sessions or logistical meetings. They're simple opportunities to see each other, voice frustrations before they build up, and stay in sync as a parenting team. If you feel like ships passing in the night, check-ins can bring you back together.

Finding time is tough, but it pays off. Try weekly or bi-weekly "state of the union" chats to keep communication open. Fifteen minutes after bedtime or a quiet coffee while the baby naps can make a difference. These moments don't have to be formal; a chat on the porch or a walk with the stroller works. What's crucial is showing up intentionally, not just as household managers, but as co-captains of your family.

A structure keeps things productive and relaxed. Three prompts help: "What's working?" "What's tough?" and "What could we try differently?" This focus prevents blame or old fights from resurfacing. Truly listen to your partner's answers, don't interrupt or rush to fix things. Sometimes all that's needed is acknowledgment: "Yeah, that's been hard." Share your own wins and struggles honestly as well. If you're stretched thin or unsure how to help, say so. The goal isn't perfection, but connection.

Appreciation holds everything together. Don't just dwell on negatives; call out the small things your partner did well, whether it's being patient at 3 a.m. or handling a meltdown at the store. Positive feedback isn't cheesy; it keeps you both going.

Check-ins don't need to look the same every time. Catch up while walking, texting, or sharing takeout after bedtime. For extra-busy days, a quick "How are you really doing?" text or shared notebook entry keeps the door open. If sitting down together feels too hard, even a brief voice memo helps.

Real life interrupts. Fatigue gets the better of you. Sometimes you'll miss a week or end up arguing. That's normal, don't let it stop you. Try using a phrase like, "Can we pause and come back to this tomorrow?" or "I love you, even if I'm grumpy." Resetting doesn't mean avoiding problems, but making space for repair.

Low-pressure talks are sustainable. If you're tired, keep it short: "What's one thing that worked for us this week?" Or ask directly, "What do you need from me right now?" Always end on something positive, a thank you, a high-five, or a laugh about some parenting mishap. Even when things are chaotic, celebrating one "dad win" (or "team win") can shift your mindset and remind you why you're doing this together.

Scheduling regular check-ins builds trust and teamwork, even in the chaos. You'll spot patterns before resentment sets in, and feel less isolated. These check-ins aren't just for venting; they help you celebrate wins, brainstorm small adjustments, and remember you're partners as well as parents.

Quick Check-In Template

- What's working this week?

- What's been tough?

- What could we try differently next week?

- Anything you want to appreciate about each other?

- End with a team win or a laugh.

Don't stress if some weeks are clunky or interrupted by the baby or work. What matters is that you keep showing up, making adjustments, and giving your relationship space to grow.

In the end, this chapter isn't about perfect balance; it's about staying genuinely connected through messy, real effort. You won't always get it right, but building habits of presence, teamwork, and honest conversation will help you navigate the wild first year. Next up: we'll dive into money, gear, and growing together as a family, so you can feel ready for whatever comes next.

CHAPTER 8
Money, Gear, and Growing as a Family

Budget Reality Check: What You Really Need (and What's Hype)

The first time I saw a "baby registry must-haves" list, I laughed, and then panicked. You might know the feeling: standing in a store, overwhelmed by shelves of gear promising to make you a better parent and your baby safer or happier. Most of us want to give our kids everything, but there's a big difference between what's truly needed and what's just clever marketing. This distinction is easy to lose track of, especially when you're exhausted and anxious to do things right.

Let's get honest about the actual costs. The first year with a baby can be expensive, but it doesn't have to break the bank. Most new parents spend $200–$400 per month. Diapers and wipes alone cost about $50–$80 monthly if you use disposables. Formula can add $80–$150 more per month if you're not exclusively breastfeeding. Basic clothing costs about $20–$40 a month, given growth spurts and inevitable messes. Pediatrician visits sneak up, even with good insurance, you'll want to budget $20–$50 each month for these.

There are always hidden expenses. Babies create mountains of laundry, so expect to buy more detergent and pay higher utility bills from extra washing. Cleaning supplies, gentle soaps, disinfectant wipes, suddenly become household staples. Even your heating or cooling bills may rise as you try to keep your baby comfortable. Nightlights, white noise machines, and other little things add up, so count on $30–$50 more monthly for these "invisible" categories.

So what's worth your money? Start with an honest "must-have" versus "nice-to-have" list. Essentials are a safe, *new* car seat, a crib or bassinet that meets safety standards, and a reliable thermometer. You'll want five to seven simple onesies, two sleep sacks or swaddles (if recommended for non-rollers), a practical baby bathtub, a few bottles (even if breastfeeding), and a pack of burp cloths. Skip extras like wipe warmers (they cool fast), and designer shoes or fancy outfits (babies outgrow them quickly and can't walk). Wait on swings, bouncers, or high chairs until you know what your baby likes; not every child cares about gadgets.

Don't tackle your baby budget alone. Community swaps and "buy nothing" groups are treasure troves for gently used baby gear, clothes, and toys, especially things only needed for a short window.

Borrowing from friends or family is common and welcomed; most are glad to pass things along, and you'll do the same one day. Consignment shops are smart if you need strollers, carriers, or bouncers; you can find like-new gear for much less. When in doubt, just ask: "Do you have any baby stuff you're done with?" People are usually relieved to declutter.

Here are a couple of real-world examples. Josh and his partner managed on a tight $50/month baby budget by using cloth diapers, hand-me-down clothes, and a borrowed bassinet. Their splurges were a new car seat and quality bottles. Another friend with twins spent closer to $150/month because of formula and double sets of essentials, but saved by joining local swap groups for toys and clothes.

Sample "bare-bones" monthly budget for a family of three:

- Diapers and wipes: $60

- Formula/Breastfeeding accessories: $100

- Basic clothes: $25

- Medical copays: $30

- Laundry/cleaning: $20

- **Total:** $235/month

If your situation allows wiggle room to splurge, pick your battles. A comfy carrier or blackout curtains can make life easier.

Interactive Element: Quick "Must-Have vs. Hype" Checklist

- Safe car seat (new): Must-have

- Crib/bassinet: Must-have

- Five+ onesies: Must-have

- Thermometer: Must-have

- Baby bathtub: Must-have

- Swings/bouncers: Wait and see

- Wipe warmer: Skip it

- Designer outfits/shoes: Skip it

- High chair: Wait until solids

- Changing table: Nice-to-have (a sturdy surface works too)

- White noise machine: Nice-to-have if it helps sleep.

As your child grows, your priorities will shift, and you'll learn what actually helps. Don't let social media or marketing pressure you; your baby really just needs you a lot more than any gadget.

Navigating Insurance, Paperwork, and Financial Surprises

Adding a new baby to your health insurance feels like a game of beat-the-clock, especially when you're running on zero sleep. Hospitals hand you forms while you're still in a daze. Bills trickle in weeks later, just when you think you're catching up. The clock starts ticking the minute your baby arrives. Most insurance companies give you 30 days, sometimes 60, to get your child added to your policy. Miss that window and you might be stuck waiting months for open enrollment or paying out of pocket for every tiny cough and checkup.

As soon as you have that birth certificate, reach out to your employer's HR or your insurance provider, even if you're still living in pajamas. Ask them straight: "What's my deadline for adding my baby?" and "What documents do I need?" It's worth getting crystal clear on deductibles, copays, and what counts as an in-network provider. Sometimes, a pediatrician you met in the hospital isn't covered by your plan, and surprise bills can spiral from there.

Paperwork is relentless in the first year. You'll need to order your baby's birth certificate, usually from the hospital or your state's vital records office. Next comes the Social Security application, which many hospitals can submit for you. If not, you'll have to do it at the local office or by mail, and you'll need that number for everything from insurance to tax returns. Pediatrician offices want copies of both, along with your insurance card, before the first well-baby visit.

Make a digital folder: scan these documents, save them to a password-protected spot (like cloud storage), and keep paper copies in a fire-safe box or locked drawer. Store immunization records and visit summaries there too. When the daycare paperwork starts rolling in, you'll thank yourself for being organized.

You'll get hit with unexpected costs; nobody warns you how fast they add up. Maybe your baby spikes a fever on a weekend and you end up at urgent care, only to find out they're out-of-network. That bill arrives, and it's way more than you expected. Or maybe there's a prescription that isn't fully covered, or a specialist visit for something minor that insurance only partially pays for. Then there are those extra childcare hours when work runs late or your sitter cancels last minute. Some expenses are just impossible to predict: extra formula when breastfeeding gets tricky, or backup glasses after a pair gets snapped in half during tummy time. You can't plan for everything, but building an emergency fund, just \$20–\$30 tucked away each month, can soften the blow when these surprises hit.

Communicating with insurance companies and HR departments can feel like decoding ancient scripts. When you write an email, be direct: "Hi, I just had a baby and need to add them to my health insurance policy. Can you confirm the steps and documents required? Is there a specific deadline?" If something doesn't make sense on a bill, don't hesitate to call or email back: "Can you explain this charge? Was this provider in-network? Is there any way to appeal this amount?" Keep every reply in your digital folder—screenshots, PDFs, even photos of paperwork if needed.

Organizing bills is half the battle. Use a simple spreadsheet or calendar app to log what's due, what you've paid, and what's still outstanding. List the date of service, provider, billed amount, what insurance paid, and what's left for you. This makes it easier to spot mistakes or overcharges. If you catch an error (and they happen often), call billing right away: "I believe there may be a mistake on this bill. Can we review it together?" Document every conversation: who you spoke with, the date, and any reference numbers.

Templates and Trackers

For insurance questions: Subject: Adding Newborn to Health Insurance

Hi [HR/Provider Name],

I recently welcomed a new baby and need to add them to my health insurance plan. Could you please confirm what steps I should take and which documents are required? Also, what is the deadline for this process?

Thank you!

[Your Name]

For bill tracking:

Date	Provider	Billed	Insurance Paid	You Owe	Paid?	Notes
6/10	Dr. Smith	$150	$120	$30	Yes	Well check

Keep this tracker on your phone or computer and update it after every bill.

When contesting a bill: "Hi [Billing Department], I have a question regarding this charge from [date]. According to my insurance statement, this should be covered at [percentage]. Can we review this together and check for errors? Please let me know if any additional paperwork is needed from my end."

You'll never remember every detail in the fog of new parenthood, but having steps written down and using scripts when nerves hit makes things less overwhelming. You don't need to become an accountant overnight; you just need a system that lets you breathe a little easier when life gets chaotic.

Choosing Baby Gear Without Overspending

Staring at walls of baby gear, strollers, car seats, swings, gadgets with more buttons than a spaceship, can make your head spin. It's easy to get pulled into the "more is better" trap when you see the endless Instagram reels and unboxing videos showing shiny, color-coordinated nurseries. The truth is, most of that stuff collects dust or gets dumped in a closet as fast as your kid outgrows a onesie. What matters is picking gear that's actually safe, works for your day-today, and doesn't leave you regretting every swipe of your credit card.

Start with safety. Before spending a dime, check the latest safety ratings for any big-ticket items: car seats, cribs, high chairs. The Consumer Product Safety Commission website lists recent recalls and safety standards, so you can be sure you're not buying something with a hidden hazard. Look for clear labels, simple harnesses, and sturdy construction. Don't skip this step. Never trust only online reviews or marketing hype; those five-star ratings might come from folks who never crash-tested a car seat in a real accident or tried to wrangle a screaming baby into a tricky harness at 3 a.m. When possible, "test-drive" strollers and car seats in-store. Snap the buckles, fold them up, lift them with one arm, see if they fit your car trunk or your actual strength level. You'll thank yourself the first time you have to pop open a stroller one-handed while holding coffee and wrangling a diaper bag.

When it comes to buying, borrowing, or waiting, use a simple decision matrix. Car seats and crib mattresses are two things worth buying new if possible. Safety standards change fast, and used items may be expired or have hidden damage. Things like baby swings, bouncers, and most newborn clothes can easily be borrowed from friends or snagged secondhand. Babies often use these for just a few months before moving on, so there's no shame in passing them along. Wait on gadgets like bottle warmers or wipe dispensers until you know if your baby even cares. They may just want warm cuddles, not warm wipes.

Trading gear with friends or through community groups works wonders if you know what to look for. Inspect everything closely before bringing it home. Moldy spots on fabric? Skip it. Cracked plastic or missing screws? Not worth the risk. Car seats have clear expiration dates stamped on the bottom. Never use one past its date or after an accident. High chairs and strollers should open and close smoothly without pinching fingers or catching fabric. For clothes and carriers, check seams, snaps, and zippers for wear—babies are tough on gear but also sensitive to rough edges.

It's so easy to get swept up in marketing pressure, especially after seeing those "must-have" lists on social feeds or hearing stories about miracle products that "change everything." Most of that is just clever advertising designed to give you FOMO (fear of missing out). Focus on what works for your family's actual lifestyle instead of what looks good in a photo grid. Some families swear by high-end bassinets that rock themselves; others find their baby sleeps best in their arms or a basic crib. Think about your space, your routine, and your actual hands-on needs.

To help filter out the noise, list out your family's top three most-used baby items after a month or two. For us, it was a sturdy travel stroller (lightweight enough for subway steps), a soft wrap carrier (perfect for walks and soothing fussy evenings), and an easy-to-clean bouncer (lifesaver during solo showers). Everything else we thought we needed ended up in the closet or was donated. Ask other dads what they really use, and most will tell you the same thing: the simpler, the better.

When well-meaning friends or relatives offer gifts that don't fit your space or values, respond kindly but honestly: "Thanks so much! We're all set for now, but I'll let you know if we need anything." This simple script keeps things positive without cluttering your life with stuff you don't want or need.

Gear Swap Checklist

When swapping gear with friends or through local groups, keep this list handy:

- Check fabric for stains or mold.

- Test all buckles/snaps/zippers.

- Inspect for missing screws/parts.

- For car seats: confirm expiration date/sticker intact.

- Ask about recalls—search model numbers online.

- Wipe down surfaces before using.

- Ensure no rough edges or fraying straps.

- Trust your gut: if something feels off, pass.

Selecting baby gear doesn't mean assembling a miniature version of Babies 'R' Us in your living room. It means choosing only what truly fits your life right now and letting go of the rest, no guilt required. Your baby will remember your arms and your laughter long after they forget the brand of their first stroller.

Monthly "Dad Wins" Reflection Pages: Tracking Growth and Gratitude

There's something quietly powerful about pausing to notice the moments that would otherwise slip by. In the chaos of new fatherhood, it's so easy to focus on what you didn't do, what you forgot, or the hundred things still on your mental checklist. But if you take a few minutes every month to jot down your "dad wins," big or small, you'll start to see your own story in a whole new way. Maybe you figured out how to calm your baby's colic with your favorite playlist, or you managed to get through a rough week at work without snapping at home. Maybe you just survived a week of teething and still managed to make your partner laugh. That counts. These little victories are the glue holding this wild year together.

Try using simple prompts as anchors. Ask yourself, "What did I do well this month?" Don't be shy. Brag a little. Did you finally nail the baby carrier after a week of wrestling with straps? Did you handle the 3 a.m. fever without losing your cool? Write it down. Pick your favorite memory with your baby, maybe it was their first smile, a spontaneous giggle fit, or just a quiet morning snuggle. These are the moments that tend to fade if you don't capture them.

Sometimes it's not about milestones but about a feeling: pride after handling bedtime solo, or relief after getting everyone to sleep before midnight for once.

It helps to split your reflection into two sides: practical achievements and emotional milestones. On one side, list out what you actually did—changed every diaper, cooked a meal, survived an outing with no forgotten items. On the other side, go deeper: "What was the biggest challenge I faced and how did I get through it?" Maybe it was balancing work deadlines with family needs or managing your own frustration when nothing seemed to work. Then, "What did I discover about my baby or my partner this month?" Perhaps you noticed your baby loves silly faces more than fancy toys, or you saw how much your partner values small gestures like a surprise coffee or a quiet hug.

Make this check-in a ritual, not a chore. Some dads like to spend ten minutes alone at the end of each month, grab your phone or a notebook, and just let it flow. Others turn it into a family thing, sharing highlights and gratitude over dinner or during a quiet walk. If you're parenting with a partner, try trading reflections. Sometimes seeing yourself through their eyes reveals strengths you didn't notice. Don't worry about perfect sentences or spelling; what matters is honesty and showing up for yourself.

Over time, these reflection pages become more than just scribbles; they're proof of growth and resilience. When you're in the weeds on a hard day, flipping back to see how far you've come can be the reset your brain needs. You'll remember the first time you soothed your baby alone, or that night you figured out how to get everyone to sleep (even if only for three hours). That sense of progress matters. It builds confidence and keeps doubt from taking over.

I've heard from dads who started this ritual, unsure if it would help. One dad told me he filled out his first page thinking he'd only write "kept baby alive." But after reading back months later, he found stories he'd forgotten—a rainy Saturday spent building blanket forts, the moment his daughter reached for his hand for the first time, a hard conversation with his partner that made things better. Another dad said his monthly notes turned into bedtime stories for his toddler later on, which became their favorite end-of-day ritual.

You don't need fancy journals or apps—scraps of paper, voice memos, even text messages to yourself will do. Just keep them somewhere safe. If you want to get creative, add photos or draw doodles next to each win. Invite your partner or even older kids into the ritual as they grow; gratitude and self-recognition aren't just for babies and dads, they strengthen the whole family.

Below is a simple template to use each month:

Dad Wins Reflection Template

- What did I do well this month?

- Favorite memory with my baby:

- Biggest challenge I faced and how I handled it:

- Something new I learned about my baby or partner:

- What am I grateful for right now?

No matter how messy life gets (and it will), this practice grounds you in what's real, your effort, your presence, and the everyday magic that comes from showing up again and again.

Building Family Traditions from Year One

In the early days of parenting, it's easy to overlook how much you're shaping your family's story. Traditions aren't about grand gestures or expensive gifts; they're about the everyday rhythms, quirks, and small rituals that give your family its unique character. When you start these routines early, even if your baby isn't aware yet, you're planting the seeds for belonging and togetherness. Simple routines like Sunday pancakes or reading a favorite silly bedtime story with voices that change each month might seem minor, but they become treasured childhood memories and the backbone of your family's identity.

Marking milestones creates a shared, unique timeline. Monthly "birthday" photos with the same toy or chair provide a visual record of growth and time together. First holidays become opportunities to invent new rituals, maybe a single handmade ornament for baby's first winter holiday, a family selfie each New Year's morning, or a handprint turkey for Thanksgiving. These repeated moments matter.

The routine itself brings comfort, even when no one recalls how it started.

Traditions don't have to be time-consuming or costly; flexible and simple ones often stick best, fitting easily into busy lives. Maybe after dinner, you always take a brief family walk, even around the block in bad weather. Perhaps Friday nights become impromptu dance parties, regardless of energy or coordination. You could write your baby an annual letter summarizing their year and your hopes, saving it for them to read someday. Skip store-bought holiday décor and instead make crafts together, letting your child's scribbles take center stage on the fridge.

The most meaningful rituals are those created together. If you're parenting with a partner, find a quiet moment to discuss the kind of traditions you'd like. Reflect on what you enjoyed or disliked about your own childhood customs, and consider trying something new—a special birthday breakfast, a funny phrase before leaving the house, or a quirky new holiday routine. Don't hesitate to let go of anything that feels forced. Traditions should be about building connection, not striving for perfection. Even if your child is too young to fully understand, they'll sense the warmth and safety these routines provide.

Stories from other dads highlight the power of traditions, especially during tough times. One father started "Saturday Superhero Breakfasts," where everyone wore capes (old towels) while eating pancakes, which became a weekly anchor for both him and his son during stressful periods. Another dad wrote monthly birthday notes to his daughter, a short snapshot of her growth, which became an emotional family tradition as she got older.

Some families lean on rituals to weather hard days: making popcorn and watching old cartoons when someone's had a rough week, or lighting a candle before dinner and sharing one good thing about the day. These aren't dramatic or social-media-worthy, but their ordinariness makes them powerful, weaving everyone together. Kids latch onto all sorts of little things—a favorite song for car rides, silly nicknames only used at home, or always sitting in the same spot for storytime. Over the years, these details become part of the family's identity.

To get started, brainstorm together. Even if your partner seems uninterested or your baby is too little to participate, list five comforting or joyful things you already do (bedtime snuggles, funny morning greetings, stroller walks). Make one "official" or invent something new, like silly hat dinners once a month or simple backyard picnics every weekend. Adapt or change traditions as your family grows and interests change.

No two families will have the same rituals, and that uniqueness is what makes traditions special. Whether you're making pancakes in superhero capes or taking monthly photos in the same chair, you're building comforting rituals and a safety net of memories that will hold your family close through whatever comes next.

Spotlight Stories: Dads Redefining Fatherhood in Diverse Families

Every family has its own rhythm, and sometimes that rhythm means rewriting the rulebook. I've talked with dads from all walks of life, and what stands out is how each found a way to shape parenthood to fit their reality, not someone else's. Take Marcus, who never imagined raising his son alone but now calls his tight-knit apartment building "the village." When a friend's baby outgrew her crib, it landed in Marcus's living room before he even asked. He started doing toy swaps with neighbors, sharing books, clothes, and sometimes even splitting the cost for bigger gear. "We don't compete to have the fanciest stuff," Marcus told me. "We just make sure every kid has what they need, when they need it." He keeps a group text with single dads in his block, and they've become each other's backup for late-night runs or last-minute babysitting.

For Aaron and Leo, two dads who grew their family through adoption, the logistics were their biggest hurdle. They spent months sorting paperwork and even more time figuring out what gear would actually serve them as new parents. Instead of buying everything new, they reached out on local parenting forums and quickly discovered a network of LGBTQ+ families ready to share advice and gently used essentials. Their most creative move was hosting a "bring your favorite baby item" potluck, a gathering where friends brought food and hand-me-downs. They learned quickly that a supportive community goes further than any store credit card. Holidays became their time to blend traditions: one year, they set up a menorah next to a rainbow sock garland and started a yearly family photo in silly hats. These small rituals helped their daughter feel surrounded by love—messy, colorful, and always genuine.

Blended families face their own set of puzzles. Jamal, stepdad to two kids and now dad to a newborn, found himself learning fast how to juggle different needs and backgrounds. His crew includes his partner's parents, who moved in to help with childcare, bringing their own customs and routines into the mix. Instead of fighting for control, Jamal leaned into flexibility. Family meetings at the kitchen table became a staple; everyone got a say in everything from meal planning to chore schedules. Hand-me-downs from older siblings were celebrated. His toddler wears her brother's superhero cape while crawling under the dining table. When his in-laws introduced their favorite lullabies from another country, Jamal realized his kids were growing up with a blend of languages and stories that made their home richer.

Some dads get creative with space and money out of necessity. Raj built his son's nursery corner using cinder blocks, leftover paint, and secondhand finds from an online free group. He focused on what mattered: safe sleep space, soft lighting, and a shelf for favorite books. Decorations came from family art sessions—handprints on the wall, paper stars hung from the ceiling. Neighbors pitched in with extra storage bins or outgrown toys. That room became a patchwork of gifts and DIY fixes, but Raj says it feels more special than anything he could've bought.

Celebrating wins looks different in every home. In multigenerational families like Sofia's, where grandpa moves in and cousins drop by often, "win" might mean everyone sitting around the table for Sunday soup or surviving a week of shared colds without losing patience. Some dads join online dad groups or meet at playgrounds for monthly "dad huddles." A place to laugh about bottle mishaps or brainstorm how to split costs on big purchases. Others keep group chats alive with photos of first steps, silly faces at dinner, or just a quick check-in after a rough night.

Community anchors these stories. Whether it's a chosen family of friends, neighbors-turned-co-parents, or relatives who step in as needed, support networks grow organically around the real needs of dads and kids. Rituals evolve naturally: group birthday parties in the park where everyone brings snacks and shares supplies; video calls with faraway relatives to keep ties strong; or simply finding pride in solving everyday problems as a team.

Looking at these stories reminds me that there's no single blueprint for being "the right kind" of dad. What matters is finding your crew, however you define it, and building something real together. Whether you're co-parenting across households or gathering your people for backyard cookouts, inclusion and creativity beat any catalog-perfect nursery.

As this book draws to a close, remember: families are built on resourcefulness and connection far more than on stuff or structure. Every dad's journey looks different, but what unites all great fathers is the courage to keep showing up with love, creativity, and a willingness to learn along the way. You don't need the newest gear or a perfect plan; you need presence, patience, and heart. The stories of diverse dads remind us that there is always another way forward, one that reflects who you are and the family you are building. So take a breath, trust your instincts, and know that you already have what it takes to lead with love. Because in the end, it is not the things you buy or the plans you make, it is the way you show up that makes you the hero your child is counting on.

CONCLUSION

You made it. If you're reading this, you've survived sleepless nights, exploded diapers, baby meltdowns, and maybe even a few of your own. You've held a tiny human at 3 a.m. and wondered if you were doing anything right. But here's the truth: You are. That's not just fluff. I wrote this book because I know, deep in my bones, that dads like you don't get told that enough.

Let's circle back to why you picked up this guide in the first place. You wanted answers, sure. But more than that, you wanted to feel capable. Maybe you needed permission to step up and get in the game, or just someone to say, "Hey, you're not alone, and you're already nailing it more than you realize." That's the heart of this book. My mission was to hand you real tools, honest stories, and a big, friendly shove toward confidence. You can do this. You are vital. Your presence matters more than any perfect technique, gadget, or Instagram-worthy family photo.

So, what did we cover? A lot. We kicked things off with the wild tornado of the first 24 hours—panic, poop, and all. You learned to create a safe baby zone, set up a "dad launchpad," and use checklists so your sleep-deprived brain doesn't have to freestyle at 2 a.m. We talked about cluster feeding, tag-teaming with your partner, and the true meaning of "Dad Mode." It's not about being flawless, it's about showing up.

Then, you dove into hands-on baby care. Bottles, burping, baths, blowouts (yes, plural), and safe sleep without swaddling. You got practical hacks: keep supplies everywhere, laugh off disasters, and always have a backup shirt for yourself. We hammered home that you don't have to be an expert to be effective; action and effort matter most.

You built bonds, one ordinary moment at a time. Holding your baby close, skin-to-skin, singing off-key lullabies, inventing silly games, and making routines that are yours. We ditched the myth that connection has to be movie-magic. Real bonding grows from small, daily bits of effort: tummy time here, bedtime story there, a giggle that makes the whole hard week worth it.

Supporting your partner? We went there, too. You learned to spot the signs of postpartum struggle, offer empathy instead of fixing, and share the load at night. We talked real communication—

awkward, honest, important. You became the kind of partner who takes action, not just instructions. Teamwork isn't about tallying chores. It's about getting through the fog together, laughing at the mess, and forgiving each other (and yourself) when things get tense.

We didn't forget about you, either. Dad health matters. You learned to spot stress, use micro self-care breaks, and reach out when things get tough. You made space for your own feelings, without shame or apology, and found ways to connect with other dads. You discovered that "dad bod" isn't a punchline; it's a badge of hands-on parenting.

You learned to track milestones without losing your mind. You found out what's normal, what's not, and how to trust your gut when something feels off. You got scripts for talking to doctors, checklists for emergencies, and a reminder that every baby's timeline is unique.

We tackled work-life chaos. You built a "morning launchpad," figured out how to stay connected after paternity leave, and learned that ten-minute windows of real presence beat hours of distracted multitasking. You ditched the guilt, stopped comparing, and found ways to keep your partnership strong through check-ins and shared wins.

Money and gear? We pulled back the curtain on what's actually necessary and what's just hype. You got budgeting tips, insurance scripts, and a reality check on what matters. Your baby doesn't need a wipe warmer; they need you. And you've got this.

One thing I hope came through loud and clear: This book is for all dads. It's for the dad in sweats, the dad in a suit, the single dad, the dad with two dads, the adoptive dad, the dad who became a parent at 19, and the dad who started at 49. There's no "right" shape for a family. There's just showing up. No stereotypes, no shame, no gatekeeping. You belong here.

Let's recap some of the biggest "dad wins" you're taking with you:

- Daily care checklists that keep you sane.

- Dad hacks for chaos—like prepping stations and backup onesies.

- Teamwork rituals with your partner.

- Micro self-care routines (yes, five minutes counts).

- Milestone trackers you'll actually use.

- Creative family traditions, even if it's just Saturday pancakes or goofy bedtime handshakes.

If you remember nothing else, remember this: Progress beats perfection. Every day you show up, every time you try again, every time you laugh off a fail and try a new way, you're giving your child what they need most. You.

Keep using those reflection pages. Mark down your "dad wins" each month, no matter how small. Track milestones, not to compare, but to remember how far you and your family have come. Keep having those check-ins with your partner. Build traditions that reflect your real life, not someone else's highlight reel.

And don't keep this journey to yourself. Put the advice in this book to work. Try something new tonight. Reach out to a friend or a dad group. Ask for help when you need it. Share your stories, your real stories, the messy ones and the hilarious ones, with other dads. You'll inspire more people than you know.

If you hit a wall or you need backup, turn to the resources at the end of this book. There are helplines, online groups, and a whole bunch of dads out there ready to listen. And if you've got a "dad win" you're proud of, share it with us. Your story helps another dad believe he can do it, too.

Thank you for trusting me with your time, your worries, and your hopes. Thank you for letting me be part of your journey. I believe in every dad who picked up this book. You are already making a difference. You are exactly the hero your baby is counting on. You've got this, one day, one diaper, one dad win at a time.

As This Book Helps You With Your Baby…

Whether you learn tips on crying, swaddling, sleep, bonding with your baby, or supporting your partner, we want to hear it. Please leave a review on Amazon.

How To Review This Book:

1. Open your camera app.
2. Scan the QR code above.
3. Wow! The review page opens! (Click the link)
4. Enter a star rating.
5. Share a few words about what you think.

Photos or videos of your experience can help others see how fun and useful this book really is!

REFERENCES

- *Comprehensive Newborn Care Guide for Dads | Delaware WIC* https://delaware.wicresources.org/eat-grow-live-healthy/dads-guide-to-newborn-care/

- *Sleep-Related Infant Deaths: Updated 2022 ...* https://publications.aap.org/pediatrics/article/150/1/e2022057990/188304/Sleep-Related-Infant-Deaths-Updated-2022

- *A Partner's Support During Postpartum Can Literally Be ...* https://www.whattoexpect.com/pregnancy/for-dad/life-after-childbirth.aspx

- *How to Change a Diaper - Expert Tips on Changing a Baby* https://www.daduniversity.com/blog/how-to-change-a-diaper-expert-tips-on-changing-a-baby

- *How Dads Can Support Their Breastfeeding Partner* https://wicbreastfeeding.fns.usda.gov/how-dads-can-support-their-breastfeeding-partner

- *Sleep-Related Infant Deaths: Updated 2022 ...* https://publications.aap.org/pediatrics/article/150/1/e2022057990/188304/Sleep-Related-Infant-Deaths-Updated-2022

- *Baby bath basics: A parent's guide* https://www.mayoclinic.org/healthy-lifestyle/infant-and-toddler-health/in-depth/healthy-baby/art-20044438

- *8 Hacks for Dealing With Diaper Blowout* https://tabeeze.com/blogs/press/diaper-blowout-hacks?srsltid=AfmBOor513J1wH8ZChyx6TMu7ZqgWve59yXe8kmYnnLYkM4IcSgPXgHs

- *Prolactin, Oxytocin, and the development of paternal ...* https://pmc.ncbi.nlm.nih.gov/articles/PMC3247300/

- *Why Dads and Their Babies Need to Go Skin-to-Skin*
  https://www.scientificamerican.com/article/why-dads-and-their-babies-need-to-go-skin-to-skin1/

- *Fun Bonding Activities for Dads and Babies*
  https://childdevelopmentinfo.com/how-to-be-a-parent/fun-bonding-activities-for-dads-and-babies/

- *What to do when your baby or toddler only wants Mom …*
  https://takingcarababies.com/what-to-do-when-your-baby-or-toddler-only-wants-mom-or-dad?srsltid=AfmBOoqBUW3tnPq6uxEfwlVjvElBJN4G284aSPsheCC5SOoqT9_tLR-s

- *How to be a Supportive Postpartum Partner*
  https://boramcare.com/how-to-be-a-supportive-partner-during-postpartum/

- *Postpartum depression - Symptoms and causes*
  https://www.mayoclinic.org/diseases-conditions/postpartum-depression/symptoms-causes/syc-20376617

- *Tips for Postpartum Dads and Partners*
  https://www.postpartum.net/wp-content/uploads/2014/11/Tips-for-Postpartum-Dads-and-Partners.pdf

- *The Transition to Parenthood: Relationship Tips for New …*
  https://www.gottman.com/blog/the-transition-to-parenthood-relationship-tips-for-new-parents/

- *1 in 10 dads experience postpartum depression, anxiety*
  https://utswmed.org/medblog/paternal-postpartum-depression/

- *5 Essential Self-Care Tips for First-Time Dads*
  https://healingspringswellness.com/5-essential-self-care-tips-for-first-time-dads-nurturing-your-mental-health/

- *Help for Dads | Postpartum Support International (PSI)*
  https://postpartum.net/get-help/help-for-dads/

- *Fatherhood group sessions: A descriptive and summative …*
  https://pmc.ncbi.nlm.nih.gov/articles/PMC7756429/

- *CDC's Developmental Milestones*
  https://www.cdc.gov/ncbddd/actearly/milestones/index.html

- *Sick baby? When to seek medical attention*
  https://www.mayoclinic.org/healthy-lifestyle/infant-and-
  toddler-health/in-depth/healthy-baby/art-20047793

- *Signs of Sleep Regression in Babies and What to Do About It*
  https://www.whattoexpect.com/first-year/sleep/sleep-
  regression/

- *Tummy Time* https://www.nationwidechildrens.org/family-
  resources-education/health-wellness-and-safety-
  resources/helping-hands/tummy-time

- *Improving your work/life balance as a new dad*
  https://www.gidgetfoundation.org.au/fact-sheets/improving-
  your-work-life-balance-as-a-new-dad

- *Morning Routine Tips: Get Out the Door on Time with Kids*
  https://www.littleones.co/blogs/our-blog/the-morning-how-to-
  be-organised-and-out-the-door-on-
  time?srsltid=AfmBOorYYvZNxrhSD65hxowajx9HQmnkPzw
  yjTEyguxOlGXyCYA5wVwm

- *Tips for Planning Your Return to Work After Parental Leave*
  https://www.thebump.com/a/returning-to-work-parental-leave

- *Stress Management for Dads: How Your Mental Health ...*
  https://www.inovanewsroom.org/expert-
  commentary/2019/06/stress-management-for-dads-how-your-
  mental-health-impacts-your-kids/

- *The Ultimate First Year Baby Budget*
  https://wealthkeel.com/blog/first-year-baby-budget/

- *How do I get health insurance for my new baby?*
  https://www.uhc.com/news-articles/benefits-and-
  coverage/how-do-i-get-health-insurance-for-my-new-baby

- *Baby Checklist* https://www.cpsc.gov/s3fs-public/206%20Baby%20Safety%20Checklist_web_enNEW.pdf

- *5 Family Traditions for New Babies* https://people.howstuffworks.com/culture-traditions/family-traditions/5-family-traditions-for-new-babies.htm

ABOUT THE AUTHOR

Brad Wells is an enthusiastic advocate for involved fatherhood. With a passion for family dynamics, Brad has researched and written about the transformative journey of fatherhood. He understands the challenges and joys of expecting and caring for a new life, and his experiences have inspired him to share his insights and knowledge with new fathers.

In his latest book, *"DAD, I'M COUNTING ON YOU!: How to Be a Hero in Your Baby's First 12 Months,"* Brad blends practical wisdom with heartfelt stories to guide men through the exhilarating and sometimes overwhelming journey of first-time fatherhood. His comprehensive handbook offers invaluable support and encouragement for fathers navigating the intricacies of their baby's first year.

Brad's writing is characterized by warmth, humor, and relatability, making complex topics accessible to readers of all backgrounds. Through his work, he hopes to empower fathers to embrace their role with confidence, compassion, and a sense of adventure.

When he's not writing, Brad enjoys spending time with his family, watching Netflix, and indulging his love of magic.